What Would Boudicca Do?

E. Foley and B. Coates are editors based in London. Since working on this book they have begun to channel Elizabeth I's famed public-speaking skills and taken tips from Mrs Beeton when battling imposter syndrome. They are anything but imposters when it comes to writing. They are the bestselling authors of *Homework for Grown-Ups* (of which the *Daily Telegraph* said, 'This is an obvious candidate to take to a desert island, along with Shakespeare and the Bible'). For regular inspiration from the historic sisterhood follow: @FoleyCoates

Further praise for *What Would Boudicca Do?*:

'This charming and inspiring book is part history lesson and part call to arms. Whatever's causing you grief, rest assured that a remarkable woman of the past has gone through it first and come out on the other side. Whether it's Mae West on being body positive, Agatha Christie on getting over heartbreak or Mrs Beeton on beating impostor syndrome, there are life lessons a'plenty here.' *Red Magazine*

E. Foley & B. Coates

What Would Boudicca Do?

EVERYDAY PROBLEMS SOLVED BY HISTORY'S MOST REMARKABLE WOMEN

Illustrated by Bijou Karman

FABER & FABER

First published in 2018
by Faber & Faber Limited
Bloomsbury House
74–77 Great Russell Street
London, WC1B 3DA
This paperback edition first published in 2019

Typeset by Faber & Faber Limited
Printed in the UK by CPI Group (UK) Ltd, Croydon, CR0 4YY

A CIP record for this book
is available from the British Library

ISBN 978–0–571–34049–1

2 4 6 8 10 9 7 5 3

For Jeanie, Leo
Barney, Lola, Iris and Joseph

Contents

Introduction

If you could live in any period of history which would you choose? Maybe the mystical civilisation of the ancient Egyptians? The revolutionary Renaissance of the sixteenth century? The glamorous *Mad Men* stylishness of the 1960s? The only fly in the ointment when considering your options is that you need to be a rich guy to choose any day but the present as the best possible time to be alive. For women, any of those hundreds of centuries before the twentieth looks like a bum deal, given that you wouldn't be able to do basic things like vote, be properly educated, or choose your romantic partner independently.

This book came about as the result of a mistake. We were having such a nice time bobbing along in our little bubble of progress that we thought that everything nowadays was hunky-dory for the ladies. Then the news started to rain a little on our happy feminism-has-won parade. Suddenly misogyny seemed to be hip again (Weinstein and Pussygate being two choice examples), and we found ourselves looking anxiously to the past for reassurance and inspiration: reassurance that the world is still getting more female-friendly; and inspiration from the outstanding women who beat the system way back when. Happily, we got both.

The result of our delving is this pocket guide to our heroic sisters, who, living in much tougher times, took control of their destinies and made the world work for them. Surely if women living in the days of full-on, unapologetic sexist oppression could find a way to shine and flourish, then we can too. We started talking to each other about some of the women who made history despite the fact that most of that *his*tory was recorded and peopled by rich dudes. These ladies – the Elizabeth Is and Cleopatras – led us to other, lesser-known examples of female success in ye olden days, like Fanny Cochrane Smith, Wang Zhenyi and Sophia Duleep Singh.

We discovered that things were much more serious, and more likely to end in untimely death, for the sassy women of the past, but that is not to deny that there are new and different challenges to negotiate today. Life can be troublesome for the modern gal: we're swimming the shark-infested waters of social media, constantly fiddling with the scales of our work–life balances, being actively encouraged to hate ourselves when we look in the mirror in the hope that we'll buy more sportswear, and all the while dealing with the shadow of centuries of patriarchal oppression that have also given us mansplaining/-spreading/-terrupting, and worse. Feminism's job is certainly not over, but at least we, unlike many of the ladies in this book, live in a world where it's been invented.

We all need our lodestars to steer by when things get a little dark. Our friends, mothers, sisters and colleagues can shine a light on our problems, and many of us will have asked ourselves the question 'What Would Beyoncé Do?' when faced with tests in our personal and professional lives, but Queen Bey is not the only fiercely inspiring example available to us. We can turn to the most celebrated women throughout history for advice; those sisters who led the way in the fields of science, politics and the arts, who excelled at invention, creativity and generally getting shit done.

What wisdom might Boudicca, Cixi or Sappho be able to impart from the furthest stretches of misty time? They lived in ages when underwear wasn't even a thing and livestock was prized somewhere just above women in the pecking order. None of them would have the first clue about what to do with a smartphone, but we realised that they were all trying to make their way in conditions that have many resonances today. History is a continuum, and even in vastly different circumstances, women have had families to deal with, wanted to be fulfilled by their work and worried about what they look like. In our research we saw women being underestimated at every turn, dealing with unrealistic ideals of body image, being overloaded with housework, standing up to bullies, grappling with relationships . . . The list goes on. And it's been weirdly reassuring that whether we're in Ancient Egypt or the Golden Age of the Russian Empire, frontierland America or wartime Paris, our utterly unique women have a shared experience.

We were fascinated to see that many of the same themes came up in their stories: as children they often had parents who educated them 'like boys' (i.e. beyond embroidery), but many of them also had their schooldays interrupted by their duty to look after their families; lots of them found fame with different names to those they were given at birth; many of them were sexually unconventional for their times; and most of them were true strivers – working hard and putting up with a lot of haters to get where they wanted to be. Everything is #inspiring these days, but the more we talked about these broads the more we felt fired up and empowered by their message.

We fell in love with women like scientist and gambler Ada Lovelace, who survived an acrimoniously broken home to put herself at the vanguard of modern computing; we channelled Elizabeth I's dope public-speaking skills when we were called on to give presentations at work; we took tips from the fabulous Frida Kahlo on the importance of finding our style, and why it isn't just superficial to do so. We looked at how these women handled assertiveness, failure, cack relationships, girlfriends, grief, impostor syndrome, cheating, children (or not), political engagement and the really important stuff like FOMO and appreciating their boobs. And we *were* inspired! And we learned so much! Did you know that a near-fatal bus accident caused Frida Kahlo to abandon her dreams of being a doctor and focus on painting instead? That Odette Sansom, the French housewife who was awarded the George Cross for her heroic efforts as a member of the Special Operations Executive, fell into espionage as a result of epistolary error? That pioneer domestic goddess Mrs Beeton in fact plagiarised most of her early recipes from her readers, and was pretty hopeless in the kitchen?

Our women are flawed and fabulous, and it can't be claimed that they led perfect lives, but all of them were extraordinary in their own kick-ass ways. So join us on our tour round the stereotype-smashing supergirls of history and let their stories help you conquer today.

Boudicca
and
Sticking Up for Yourself

(d. 61 CE)

Tired of being talked over in meetings? Of having your patronising boss bropropriate your ideas and present them as his own? Women have been putting up with this nonsense for countless centuries and resisting it for just as many. Faced with this kind of insult, Norfolk's famous flame-haired queen would likely have responded: 'Incinerate him!' Queen B. was the legendary chief of the Iceni tribe, who lived in East Anglia two thousand years ago. After the Romans, at the behest of their Emperor Claudius, invaded Britain in 43 CE, they made a treaty with Boudicca's husband generously allowing him to continue to govern his people. However, when he died, this gentleman's agreement didn't extend to the ladies. The Romans took Boudicca's kingdom and, according to their historian Tacitus, raped her daughters and flogged her. Instead of being cowed by this vile outrage, or simply accepting the inevitable sexual violence women endure in war zones, Boudicca set the world on fire. She led a full-on revolt in 60 or 61 CE, mercilessly burning the key settlements of Colchester, St Albans and London to the ground, slaughtering their citizens, both Roman and Briton, and seriously diminishing the crack Ninth Legion. This murderous monarch left her mark, literally, in the layer of burnt red sediment that you'll find even today if you dig down deep enough in the cities she razed.

The offences against Boudicca are clearly far more serious and unforgiveable than not being given credit in your workplace, but her emphatic response is something to be emulated, albeit with slightly less disembowelling and arson. Next time someone's stealing your sunshine, make a claim for what's yours and refuse to be disrespected. Boudicca nurtured a very literal take-no-prisoners attitude, but she is a source of encouragement for the many of us who struggle with assertiveness and the cultural pressure that pushes women to be conciliatory and likeable at all times. This ginger warrior wasn't worried about making enemies, or causing a scene, and her confident authority meant her tribe, and others, rallied around her cause.

We can't claim that Boudicca herself had a happy ending: her audacious rebellion was eventually put down at the Battle of Watling Street. Those pesky Romans turned out to be pretty good at fighting after all (as well as at road construction, aqueducts, legal systems and underfloor heating) and their superior military tactics and clever use of the terrain saw them end up on top. Boudicca is said to have committed suicide to avoid the shame of capture, characteristically both living and dying on her own terms. To add insult to injury, her name has for many centuries been spelled and pronounced wrongly – as Boadicea –

because of a typo in one of Tacitus' manuscripts.

Boudicca's name, whichever way you write it, is thought to come from the Celtic word for 'victory' and so is the equivalent of the slightly less exciting Victoria. In a pleasing quality-queen fan club, the more recent Queen Victoria (see p. 289), and before her Queen Elizabeth I (see p. 175), kept the flame of her memory alive as part of their personal propaganda in their own reigns. Liz, when stirring her troops against the Armada, wore a Boudicca-inspired outfit, and Vic named a battleship after her. Without them it is possible that B.'s feats would have been lost in the mists of time. Her reputation lives on because she categorically refused to be swept aside without a fight by the more powerful forces at play around her. It may still feel like a man's world out there but, with a lot more of us girding our G-strings, speaking up and leaning in, perhaps the day will come when the patriarchy doesn't automatically prevail.

Legend has it that Boudicca is buried on a site that falls between platforms nine and ten of King's Cross Station (one can only imagine what she makes of her bones being rattled by the *Hogwarts Express*). However, if you're looking to pay your respects, and meditate upon her resolute and decisive brilliance, the best place to commune with her fiery spirit (in the city she once torched) is by Thomas Thornycroft's Westminster Bridge statue of her belting along in her infamously weaponised, yet sadly apocryphal, chariot.

Despite being Team Roman, Tacitus gave Boudicca credit for her rousing oratory, quoting her at the Battle of Watling Street: 'On this spot we must either conquer, or die with glory. There is no alternative. Though a woman, my resolution is fixed: the men, if they please, may survive with infamy, and live in bondage.' Boudicca endures both as a symbol of resistance and as a feminist icon who confronted masculine aggression with violence at a time when this was way out of a lady's lane.

Mary Wollstonecraft
and
Calling Yourself a Feminist

(1759–1797)

Feminists. Humourless shrieky sirens who don't want us to wear bikinis, cuddle babies, bake cakes, plan weddings or decorate our stuff with cute unicorns. FFS. Simmer down, kids, it's all OK. It turns out there's been a massive misunderstanding: feminism just means equality for all genders. That's all. Feminists don't want us to be excluded from democracy, to get paid less than guys for the same job, or to get blamed for own rapes. We can get on board with that.

Sadly things aren't equal yet: one in five women in the UK will get sexually assaulted; working women earn 82p for every £1 men earn; worldwide, the pay gap isn't due to close until 2186; women's stuff in shops costs 37 per cent more than the same stuff for men; FGM is still practised. We could go on. Clearly, the fight still needs to be fought, though we don't deny that feminism has become a complex and loaded term over the years since women started to request their rights. And we have sympathy with those who want to distance themselves from the more moon-cuppy or man-hatey ends of the spectrum. To some extent it's just a question of vocabulary (some prefer to call themselves 'egalitarians'), but it is important to keep the continuity with the past that comes with this ever-vexed term. Only through this can we trace what people like Beyoncé, Sheryl Sandberg, Chimamanda

Ngozi Adichie, Caitlin Moran, Malala and Emma Watson do today, back to the work of campaigners like Emmeline Pankhurst (see p. 79), Akiko Yosano (see p. 37), Sheila Michaels (see p. 193) and the mother of 'em all, Mary Wollstonecraft.

Our Mary was born in London to a drunk, fist-happy father who squandered the family's money, and a mother who favoured her older brother (the only one of the seven children to be educated). Mary left home to work in Bath when she was nineteen and later set up a progressive school for girls with her sister and her best pal Fanny. When this fell apart, she moved to Ireland to work as a governess for some unpleasant aristos who fired her. Back in London, she started working as an editorial assistant, writer and translator for the publisher Joseph Johnson. Johnson was a radical who hung out with lots of exciting Enlightenment types, such as Thomas Paine, and the Williams Blake, Wordsworth and Godwin. In 1787 Mary published *Thoughts on the Education of Daughters*, based on her teaching experience. This was to mark the beginning of a fruitful but all too brief writing career.

In 1789 the French Revolution threw everyone into a spin and Mary joined the political fray with the publication of *A Vindication of the Rights of Men* (1790), defending civil liberties. She followed this with the companion volume *A Vindication of the Rights of Woman* in 1792, which became her most famous and influential work. It was a pioneering argument for the equal education of women so that they could contribute as much to society as men. In it she wrote: 'I shall first consider women in the grand light of human creatures, who, in common with men, are placed on this earth to unfold their faculties.' This was strong stuff for the period and a first step towards proper debate about women's rights. (For context, we are talking about an age where women couldn't own property or have custody of their own children or attend university.) Mary's argument was controversial: in a prefiguring of the style of insult pelted at feminists ever since, the writer Horace Walpole called her 'a hyena in petticoats'.

In 1792 Mary moved to France to write about the Revolution first-hand, just before it got totally terrifying and head-choppy. She fell in love with a bad boy, Gilbert Imlay, and they had a daughter, Fanny, in 1794. When the dastardly Imlay dumped her, Mary returned to London, where she attempted suicide. The next year she threw herself into a bizarre and dangerous mission in Scandinavia to try to retrieve some smuggled silver belonging to Imlay, with just her baby and maid in tow. She wrote a great book about it but that didn't solve anything with Gilbert.

Mary was once again moved to try to end it all by jumping off Putney Bridge.

By 1796 she'd recovered from Imlay and started seeing the philosopher William Godwin. They married when they discovered Mary was up the duff, despite their mutual misgivings about the institution of matrimony. They continued to live separately but to all intents and purposes had a happy and serene relationship, until the day of the birth of their child. This gave the world the baby girl who would grow up to be the super-talented author of *Frankenstein*, but caused her mother's death from complications. Inadvertently, Mary's bereaved husband proved unhelpful to the cause when he published a memoir about her in 1798, which publicised the illegitimacy of her first child and her suicide attempts. The scandal about her personal life diverted attention away from her ground-breaking work, which was not fully appreciated until many years later.

It wasn't easy being Mary but there was definitely something about her – she was a sensitive, passionate soul, who had to overcome a lot, but she always said what she thought, and had the confidence to try to change the world: 'I have a heart that scorns disguise, and a countenance which will not dissemble.' Even after her death the unsisterly sniping and gossiping about the links between her morals and her colourful personal life endured, with many blaming her daughters' fates (Fanny committed suicide and Mary Jnr skipped off with the poet Percy Bysshe Shelley) on the example she set. The haters are always going to hate, but this is nothing to be afraid of. The concept of feminism didn't really exist when Mary lived her feminist life, but don't you think we owe it to her to get in formation and embrace it now?

Mae West
and
Being Body Positive

(1893 – 1980)

Courgette spaghetti, avocado 'chocolate' mousse, desiccated kale crisps: the low-carb, clean-eating, wellness-expert money train has a lot to answer for. We're all for good nutrition and keeping fit but it can be exhausting keeping up with society's (and our own) unrealistic expectations of how we should look. Professional actresses and models may spend all their time hot piloxing* and nibbling on steamed spinach, but there's no way the rest of us can match the genetics, expense and time that having 'looking good' as a job requires. If you're ever feeling down with your dumpiness, remember the wise words attributed to callipygous cynosure and Hollywood legend Mae West: 'A curve is the loveliest distance between two points.'

Mary Jane West was born in Brooklyn. Her mother was a model and her father was a boxer who built mini-Mae her own stage at home. Aged twelve she started working in vaudeville, singing and dancing, sometimes in drag, and she was only eighteen when she made her Broadway debut, where her performance was praised by the *New York Times*. (She also secretly married some random called Frank at this point: they very swiftly separated, but only finally divorced

---

* A brutal cross between Pilates and boxing, performed wearing heavy gloves and to pumping beats.

in 1943 when the press found out about him.) Mae continued to blossom on Broadway and in nightclub shows until her breakthrough in 1926.

Mae wrote and produced the bluntly titled *Sex*, in which she played a prostitute. The show was a scandalous success and after over three hundred performances the authorities decided they'd had enough. The play was closed down and Mae was arrested for obscenity and corrupting the morals of the youth. Canny Mae knew that all publicity was definitely good publicity and she exploited the trial and her subsequent eight-day imprisonment to the max, cementing her reputation as a sexually liberated iconoclast. She hired a limo to take her to jail and told everyone she wore her best silk undies throughout her stay. Khloé Kardashian eat your heart out. After her release, she used the cash from a magazine interview about her experience to set up a library in the prison. This was a fitting endowment for a woman whose favourite pastime, aside from sex and winding up the pearl-clutching moralists of her time, was writing. She wrote more successful plays after *Sex*, including *The Drag* (which was supportive of homosexuality and banned after ten shows), *Diamond Lil* (1928) and *The Constant Sinner* (1931).

Mae was a great wit, both on the page and in person. She became notorious for imbuing every sentence

21

she spoke with a sparkle of salacious smuttiness and she knew how to work her attractive, curvaceous figure to exacerbate this effect. Mae was just over five feet tall and famously well upholstered, to the point that World War II sailors called their lifejackets 'Mae Wests'. She was immensely proud of her body, even if it didn't completely fit with the fashion of her time, where a leaner Joan Crawford physique was in vogue. In later life she installed a mirror over her bed, filled her house with pictures of herself and adorned her piano with her own naked statue.

In the tales of Hollywood starlets hitting the big time, Mae's is unusual. She was a positively ancient thirty-eight when she was signed by Paramount studios, she wrote her own lines (until the censors came down on her), picked her own co-stars and was happy to be perceived as a risqué, salty kind of dame. The movies *Night after Night* (1932) and *She Done Him Wrong* (1933) saved Paramount from bankruptcy and made her the highest-paid woman in the US. However, in the later 1930s her scripts were compromised by increasingly nervy censorship wusses: even though none of her films contained anything we'd consider remotely provocative. In contrast to the pornified free-for-all of today, Mae's sauciness was all in the implication. In *Night After Night* a woman says to her, 'Goodness, what beautiful diamonds,' to which Mae replies, 'Goodness had nothing to do with it.' She titled her 1959 autobiography with this line.

Frustrated by Hollywood's restrictions, Mae took her talents back to the stage and to Las Vegas, where she performed surrounded by a gaggle of bodybuilders: 'A man should take as good care of his body as a woman does.' She returned to films in the 1960s. Her last movie was *Sextette* (1978), in which she utters the famous 'Is that a gun in your pocket or are you just glad to see me?' line. She died of a stroke two years later, deeply mourned by her many fans.

Mae was naturally gorgeous, and she certainly spent a lot of time making sure she looked her best, but she never kowtowed to what other people thought beauty was. She was secure in her own attractiveness – 'I never needed clothes to feel sexy. I feel that way all the time' – even though she endured dissing from ungallant men like Graham Greene and her co-star W. C. Fields, who referred to her respectively as 'an overfed python' and 'a plumber's idea of Cleopatra'. Much like the divine Cleo (see p. 119), Mae was a confident, independent woman who knew how to use her body, and men's vulnerability to its charms, to help her get what she wanted. And for Mae that tended to be work, attention and jewels: admirable goals,

23

in our opinion. She ended up an icon: Salvador Dalí designed a sofa shaped like her lips and she appears in Frida Kahlo's (see p. 85) painting 'My Dress Hangs There'. Her thrifty beauty tip was to use baby oil, warmed, and applied to the whole body by an admirer. Her nutritional advice? 'I never worry about diets. The only carrots I'm interested in are the number you get in a diamond.'

Rosa Parks
and
Standing Up to Bullies

(1893 – 1980)

Chances are you know a grandparent or parent who remembers 1955 and how life was then. We're not talking about deepest darkest history here, so it's shocking to realise how bleak things were for Alabama's black citizens just over sixty years ago. The Jim Crow laws that had sprung up in the Southern states after the American Civil War meant that public transport, restaurants, libraries and cemeteries were all segregated. Black lives were under threat from the dangerous clowns in the Ku Klux Klan, and, despite being given the vote in 1870, black citizens were still excluded in some states, including Alabama, thanks to by-laws requiring all voters to prove their literacy or tax payment. (Alabama had also only just officially ratified the 1920 constitutional amendment allowing women to vote, thirty-three years late, in 1953. Bad form, boys.) During rush hour on a December day in 1955, Rosa Parks took a stand against these injustices by keeping her seat.

Rosa Louise McCauley was born in Alabama. She had to leave school to care for her family but when she married Raymond Parks in 1932 he supported her so that she could go back and get her diploma. Like Rosa's family, Raymond was involved in the growing civil rights movement and a member of the National Association for the Advancement of Colored People

(NAACP) in Montgomery. Rosa later joined too and became Secretary of the local branch. In 1944 she worked on a nearby military base that was unsegregated, so she saw first-hand that there was a better way to live.

There was a turning point for the civil rights movement in 1954 after the Supreme Court sensibly ruled that segregated schools were unconstitutional. The NAACP saw an opportunity to challenge the policy of segregation on public transport. Buses were divided into black and white seating areas but, as if this weren't offensive enough, drivers also often insisted black passengers give up their seats for white people, even in their own section. People who disobeyed this law were subject to arrest, fines, imprisonment and violence. On 1 December 1955, Rosa was coming home from her work as a seamstress at a department store and sitting in a row with three other black passengers as the bus filled up. When a white man boarded, the driver asked Rosa's whole row to stand so the man could sit down. They all got up except for Rosa.

When the driver told Rosa he was going to call the police, she elegantly replied, 'You may do that.' She was arrested because clearly it was considered an excellent use of police time to keep an eye on where people put their asses. As a respectable, middle-aged woman, Rosa was the perfect test case for the NAACP to apply pressure to the segregation laws. They called for public solidarity in a boycott of the buses, which was immensely successful. The boycott was managed by a twenty-six-year-old pastor called Dr Martin Luther King Junior, and 98 per cent of Montgomery's black citizens – the main customer base for the service – supported it. It lasted for over a year, during which time Rosa and her supporters endured death threats, dismissal from their jobs, arrests and attacks on their homes. Eventually the Supreme Court ruled in their favour, and on 21 December 1956 Montgomery's buses were finally integrated.

The next year, having endured such a devitalising struggle, Rosa and Raymond left Alabama and moved close to Rosa's brother in Detroit, but they remained involved in the campaign for equality for people of colour in the United States. Rosa won several awards for her work and is celebrated as the mother of the civil rights movement. After her death in 2005, she became the first woman in history to lie in state at the Capitol.

Sometimes Rosa's actions are cast as a spontaneous or emotional moment of resistance, but this is to underplay how involved she was in the strategic planning of the civil rights groups as they took on the racist machinery of state governments. It's true that her bravery and uncompromising behaviour in the heat of the moment, as a black woman in a society that threatened serious violence for such actions, should be applauded, but so should her smart thinking and endurance before and after that fateful day. Rosa shows that making the right alliances and preparing carefully, as well as having the confidence to stand up for what you believe in when you are most vulnerable, will help you tough it out and get something difficult done. As the woman herself said: 'You must never be fearful about what you are doing when it is right.' And you should never nick someone else's seat on the bus.

Mina Wylie, Fanny Durack *and* the Art of Female Friendship

Wilhelmina Wylie (1891–1984)
Sarah Durack (1889–1956)

G et it right, and your relationship with your best friend can be one of the most significant of your life – and often the most supportive. Just ask Wilhelmina 'Mina' Wylie who, along with her BFF Sarah 'Fanny' Durack, swam against the tide: fighting stuffy social convention, changing the rules, and going on to achieve sporting stardom.

Born in North Sydney, Australia, Mina was lucky enough to have a dude of a dad who had been a distance diving champion and underwater performer, and she joined his aquatic act, along with her brothers, at the age of five. Her trick as part of the show was to swim with her feet and hands tied together: a move which flutterkick-started her stellar career and demonstrated breathtakingly lax parenting skills from Wylie Senior. More helpfully, her dad built Wylie's Baths at Coogee Beach, a beautiful tidal pool where she could train every day. The rules around men and women bathing together at the same time were strict; here she could paddle about as she pleased. Mina was joined there by another swimmer, Fanny Durack, and they were encouraged by Mr Wylie to train together. The girls got seriously good and won all the championships open to them. They could see the 1912 Stockholm Olympics on the horizon, and believed it was time to display their natatorial talents on a global stage.

However, there were several party-poopers ready to rain on the friends' ambitions. The primary, and somehow most perplexing, adversary, was Rose Scott, President of the New South Wales Ladies' Amateur Swimming Association and stand-out suffragette. She quit in protest when Fanny and Mina were finally selected for the Olympic team; she just couldn't bear the thought of women competing in front of men. She was convinced that male athletes were incapable of controlling themselves around ladies in swimsuits, even when said swimsuits could hardly be accused of sauciness, stretching as they did from high neck to mid-thigh. Still, all that breaststroking was guaranteed to set the cocks a-twitching in her opinion. But the Mayor of Randwick (where Wylie's Baths were located) disagreed, pointing out the manifest truth that sheilas' bodies were 'not a matter for shame or seclusion'.

Despite this mayoral support, the Australian Olympic Committee initially refused to budge, and left Mina and Fanny out of their line-up, claiming they didn't have enough money to send them to Sweden. Public outrage ensued: donations poured in, and the requisite dollars were rounded up. In the end Mina's dad went as coach and Fanny's sister as chaperone on the long ocean voyage to Europe, and together the four of them made up the first ever Australian Olympic ladies' swimming team. The bonzer bathing babes triumphed in the women's 100 metre freestyle event: Mina took silver, Fanny took gold. But there was one obstacle they couldn't overcome – they tried to prolong the party by competing in the women's 4 × 100 metre relay, but as there were only two of them it was a no-no – despite their neat suggestion that they swim two legs of the pool each. Nevertheless the girls became national heroines, capturing the hearts of the public (unlike the disappointing men's team, who seriously underperformed that year).

Mina and Fanny dedicated themselves to promoting their sport for the rest of their lives: between 1906 and 1934 Mina triumphed at 115 state and national events and defended world records in breaststroke, backstroke and freestyle, while Fanny managed, between 1912 and 1918, to smash twelve world records. After they retired, both women applied themselves to coaching youngsters – imagine the honour of being taught doggy-paddle by Australia's first female Olympians.

Amphibious amigas Mina and Fanny swam right up to the doubters and told them where to dunk it, and grabbed an Olympic medal each while they were at it. They were phenomenal women in their own right, but it's difficult to see how they could have overcome all the wet blankets in their way if they hadn't had each other's backs. The best friendships will support and inspire, will spur you on to do greater and better things and bring out your best self. True friends are the ones who know every weird bit of you and still want to hang out; they're the ones who don't require constant maintenance; they will always provide a shoulder to cry on, without worrying about your mascara ruining their new top; and they'll go after the person who made you cry in the first place. Lean on your pals: they're the ones who will provide a life-jacket when you're navigating life's choppy waters.

Akiko Yosano
and
Loving Your Boobs

(1878 – 1942)

Boobs, norks, tatas, hooters, tits, bangers, cans, puppies, melons, jugs, funbags, knockers . . . However you choose to describe them, you should love this ace part of your torso. Artists have painted them, writers have waxed lyrical about them. But as Akiko Yosano shows in her sexy poetry, the aesthetics aren't what count; it's a woman's relationship to her own body that we should be celebrating. Whether big or small, your boobs are a source of power – they are life-giving (six-month-old humans can live off them exclusively), a source of sexual pleasure (your own, not just your partner's), and a tool in seduction (bizarrely, the idea of buying fancy underwear to show off blokes' hairy ballbags is unfashionable) and protest (FEMEN rock the bare-breasted look).

The significance and symbolism of breasts have metamorphosed through history and geography (the woman most often depicted with her tits out in the West is probably The Nursing Madonna herself, rather than any glamour model). At different times and in different places they have been considered, usually by men, as primarily nurturing, sexy or entirely uninteresting (in cultures where the norm is to leave them uncovered). Akiko Yosano was noted for being the first female poet in Japan to refer to them explicitly and associate them with a woman's identity and sexuality. Akiko was born near Osaka, the daughter of a sweetshop owner. If that sounds like every kid's dream, the harsh truth is that both her parents were gutted that she was a girl. She was apparently a difficult, shy and imaginative child. By the time she hit her teenage years, and started dressing up in bold, brightly coloured kimonos which set her apart from the crowd, it was clear she did not intend to be an 'ordinary' traditional woman only good for domestic chores and churning out kids.

Akiko grew up in a time of change for Japan. In the seventeenth century, the country had closed its borders to foreign trade to combat exploitation and pesky Christian evangelism from the West. But in 1853, Commodore Perry had arrived with his boats and bullied Japan into becoming buddies with the US. Outside influence began to creep in for the first time in two hundred years and Akiko embraced it, whilst at the same time paying homage to classical Japanese literary tradition in her work.

Akiko read widely and wrote her first poems when she was sixteen, sometimes while managing the sweetshop. She wrote *tanka* (kind of like *haiku* but with a different syllable pattern), joined a writing group and started publishing her work in magazines. One of these was *Myōjō*, an influential literary rag set up by the poet Tekkan Yosano. In 1900 Akiko and

Tekkan began pen-palling, and when they eventually met Tekkan became her mentor (see Althea Gibson on p. 169). Despite his existing wife and child, Tekkan and Akiko moved to Tokyo together and married in 1902. They had thirteen children, which is impressive enough, but both also continued to produce exceptional literary work, with Akiko eventually outshining her husband. She apparently often composed her poems while doing housework in an impressive display of multi-tasking and work–life fusion.

Akiko's first book was a collection of 399 *tanka* called *Midaregami* (*Tangled Hair*). The majority are love poems to Tekkan. Over the course of her life she wrote twenty books, many essays and published translations. Her poems were sensational because they moved the refined *tanka* form on to something far more frank, expressive and passionate and were often about art, individualism and women's relationship with their own bodies:

> Pressing my breasts
> I softly kick aside
> the Curtain of mystery
> How deep the crimson
> of the flower here.

Here Akiko is talking about her breasts as belonging purely to her and as contributing to her pleasure. This was pretty punchy for a society where arranged marriage was still common and women were encouraged to be nice and quiet. The establishment was predictably appalled. She also courted controversy with other intimate poems about relationships and childbirth such as:

> I am all alone,
> totally, utterly, entirely on my own,
> gnawing my lips, holding my body rigid,
> waiting on inexorable fate.
> There is only one truth.
> I shall give birth to a child,
> truth driving outward from my inwardness.
> Neither good nor bad; real, no sham about it.

(On the same subject she also commented: 'It is strange that among those men who debate women's issues, there are those who view women as being physically weak. What I want to ask these people is whether a man's body could bear childbirth?') Her 1904 poem 'Brother, Do Not Die', in which she worried about her soldier sibling dying in the Russo-Japanese war, also caused a brouhaha. She was roundly criticised for being unpatriotic, but the poem was taken up by the pacifist cause.

In her essays, Akiko argued for better lives for women, and she also worked with the controversial early feminist magazine *Seitō* (*Bluestocking*), which was set up in 1911. Women associated with the mag were slammed for wearing Western dress, going out together and smoking – much like the ladettes of the 1990s. While living at home Akiko had encouraged her parents to give her little sister a better education than she had received, and in 1921 she co-founded the girl's school Bunka Gakuin in Tokyo. When Tekkan died Akiko turned to poetry to express her grief. Heart problems led to her own death in 1942, and she slipped out of the limelight until the next decade, when she was rediscovered both as a poet and an early Japanese feminist.

Yes, we still live in a society where boobs can be controversial – Page 3, nip-slips, Facebook's breastfeeding pic ban, *Vogue*'s 2016 piece declaring them unfashionable – but you should feel free to write as much poetry about them as you like. Whether you choose to get them out or cover them up, breasts should never be a source of aesthetic anxiety. They are to be celebrated as part of a woman's life – big or small, funny-shaped or perfectly proportioned, surgically created, enhanced or diminished. Embrace them, celebrate them, own them. And for the sake of their health, make sure you give them a good feel-up every month after your period to check all is ship-shape and Bristol fashion.

Chevalier d'Éon
and
Bending the Gender Rules

(1728–1810)

The spectacularly monikered Charles-Geneviève-Louise-Auguste-Andrée-Timothée de Beaumont, the Chevalier d'Éon, lived a life full of drama and reversals of fortune. Sometimes a Chevalier and sometimes a Chevalière, so many stories abound around this illustrious Frenchperson's biography that it is hard to know what is fact and what is gossipy embellishment. For starters, apparently Mama d'Éon dressed her child as a girl until the age of seven even though the youngster was regarded as a son by Papa, who needed a male heir for inheritance purposes. This tale sets the theme that runs through much of d'Éon's notoriety.

The d'Éons were reasonably posh, but not rich, and Charles came to rely on the patronage of a close pal, King Louis XV's cousin, the Prince de Conti. Conti unlocked an extremely interesting career path for the Chevalier in *le Secret du Roi* – the King's spy network that worked behind the back of the official government. Charles was sent to Russia to clandestinely build bridges with the Empress Elizabeth (see Catherine the Great on p. 205), side-stepping the obstructions of her courtiers by dressing as a woman and infiltrating her entourage of female companions. The mission was successful and, after leaving Russia in 1760, Charles fought as a man in the Seven Years' War, a conflict which ended in defeat for France in

44

1763. King Louis quickly deployed his spies into the corridors of power of his victorious arch-enemy, Britain. Our secret agent ended up in the thick of it as secretary to the French ambassador in London. Charles had the honour of delivering the Treaty of Paris, formalising the end of Anglo-French hostilities (for a few years at least), to the King in Versailles.

This career highlight made Charles a bit uppity: living the high life, amassing both huge debts and a cache of official French secrets, with which our slippery spy tried to blackmail the bosses back in France into agreeing a pay rise. When this strategy failed, Charles published a book of revealing letters from the French ambassador, which caused a scandal and blushes all round. In retaliation *l'ambassadeur* spread rumours about the Chevalier's gender and instigated legal proceedings. Charles hid the controversial documents and stocked the house with gunpowder. Mad betting on whether Charles was really a man or a woman also ensued, resulting in the Chevalier, who was handy with a blade, challenging a lot of rude rumour-mongers to duels.

In 1774 Louis XV died and his grandson, Louis XVI, wanted those secret papers back and his wayward Chevalier under control. He did this by arranging a contract whereby '*la Chevalière*' would get a pension if *she* returned the papers and agreed to dress 'in the garments of her sex and never leave off wearing them'. This sudden designation of Charles as officially female was perhaps intended to discredit any secrets the Chevalière might blab and also to exclude Charles from the realms of political significance – as women obviously can't be trusted with matters of import. From 1777, the Chevalière lived as a woman and dressed exclusively in skirts and dresses. (Charles's first new outfits were put together by Marie Antoinette, queen of glamorous fash.) When the American War of Independence kicked off, Charles asked for permission to join up and fight, as a man, but was denied.

In 1785 a return to London beckoned. Money was tight, so Charles started giving spectacular fencing displays in a signature black dress to earn a crust. In 1792 Mary Wollstonecraft (see p. 13) namechecked 'Madame d'Éon' in her *Vindication of the Rights of Women* but things nonetheless continued to decline on the financial front: the French Revolution saw the end of the Chevalière's pension. Charles ended up living – and in 1810 dying – modestly, with a companion called Mrs Cole, who was extremely surprised by the autopsy report which revealed that the Chevalière was biologically a man.

Despite Charles being one of the most prominent transvestites in history, it is impossible to know exactly what, if any, gender s/he was. The bold Chevalière is included here because for over three decades of an extraordinary life Charles appears to have identified as a woman, even when the political circumstances behind the original change in gender designation had altered. Charles's legacy lives on in the somewhat archaic word 'eonism', meaning 'the adoption of feminine mannerisms, clothing, etc., by a male'. There is also a fantastic portrait in the National Portrait Gallery in London, and the Beaumont Society, which takes the Chevalière's name, gives advice on transgender issues today. Charles's exciting life and refusal to be pigeonholed one way or another – revelling in being shit-hot at the masculine art of sword-fighting while wearing a flouncy dress – is liberating. *Vive la Chevalière!*

Gráinne ní Mháille
and
Work–Life Balance

(*c.* 1530 – *c.* 1603)

Juggling is hard. Not just actual juggling, which is definitely hard, but also handling the different demands on our time. We all have responsibilities, which don't always feel cool and fun, but the key to it all is balance. Managing the obligations we owe to our jobs, friends and families is a delicate art. Who better to look to for advice on this sort of subtle, psychological challenge than a skirt-swirling, pistol-toting sixteenth-century pirate queen?

Gráinne ní Mháille (often anglicised to Grace O'Malley) was born around 1530 into a powerful Western Irish clan. Her family were skilful sailors who ran a marine protection racket off the coast around Galway Bay from their castles. Gráinne was probably born at Belclare Castle and educated on Clare Island. From an early age she was eager to stretch her wings beyond the traditional womanly duties expected of her. When she asked her parents if she could go with her father on a trading trip to Spain they shut her down, saying it wasn't appropriate for a young lady and she'd get her pretty pigtails stuck in the rigging. Gráinne immediately gave herself a transformative haircut and sheared off her flame-red tresses, earning herself the nickname *Gráinne Mhaol* – Gráinne the Bald – and a place on the ship.

Gráinne swiftly picked up the seafaring skills and

piratical craft that had stood her father in such good stead, but she was still expected to settle down. She was married off at the tender age of sixteen to the powerful Donal Ó Flaithbheartaigh, in a political alliance that gave Gráinne influence over a large territory centred around Bunowen Castle. Donal let her continue to hone her buccaneering prowess and she was said to keep a rope from her window to her moored ship outside to make her commute more convenient. This is the kind of death-sliding lifehack we need to emulate to keep on top of our to-do lists. Over the next nineteen years Grace had three children, Eoghan, Méadhbh and Murchadh, and travelled to Spain, Scotland and France doing business, raiding ships and generally marauding around.

These were tasty times in Irish history, as King Henry VIII started to meddle in the affairs of Éire and the clans continued to vie for supremacy. Donal was killed in an ambush in 1565 but his men continued to follow Gráinne, who by now commanded twenty ships and hundreds of sailors. Her enterprises had also started to bother the English government, who referred to her as 'a director of thieves and murderers' (always nice to see a woman gaining a director-level position). Around this time Gráinne found a shipwrecked sailor to keep her company until the bothersome MacMahons of Ballyvoy murdered him. In revenge, she sacked their castle, Doona, adding the more sinister sobriquet 'The Dark Lady of Doona' to 'the Bald' in her list of nicknames.

In 1566 Gráinne married Risdeárd Bourke – known as Iron Dick. She was more enthusiastic about Dick's castle – Rockfleet – than she was about Dick. Only one year into their marriage they separated, apparently after she yelled 'Risdeárd Bourke, I dismiss you' out of a window at him. In 1567 she also gave birth to their only son, Tiobóid, while on a sea voyage and under attack from Algerian pirates. In an admirable instance of work–life integration, and astonishing physical stamina, Gráinne inspired her troops by coming above deck wrapped in a blanket and brandishing a gun, just after producing the infant.

For Gráinne work and family were always closely intertwined as her children fought with, and sometimes against, her. In 1579 the English besieged her castle but she rebuffed them with assertive methods, including pouring boiling oil on their troops. She rebelled openly against English incursion in 1585, losing her oldest son, Eoghan, in the ensuing conflict and witnessing the treachery of her second son, Murchadh (whose lands she then burned in revenge). In 1593 her third son, Tiobóid, was captured and

Gráinne sailed to London to negotiate with Queen Elizabeth I in person (see page 175). Their meeting at Greenwich Palace was conducted entirely in Latin as neither ruler spoke the other's language. They came to a temporary agreement and Tibóid was released. Not that T. was always the apple of his mother's eye. During one battle when he was not looking terribly enthusiastic she yelled, '*An ag iarraidh dul i bhfolach ar mo thóin atá tú, an áit a dtáinig tú as?*' ('Are you trying to hide in my arse, where you came from?')

Gráinne died in Rockfleet Castle in 1603 of natural causes and is buried on Clare Island. She is remembered as a folk heroine, and even the English Lord Deputy of Ireland said she was 'famous for her stoutness of courage, and person, and for sundry exploits done by her by sea'. Gráinne was expected to put all her energies into her home life but she found a balance that worked for her – one that led her into the commercial and martial sphere of men. However, she did not neglect the ties that bound her to her family and her community and, although few of us can look to a corsairing career on the open seas for fulfilment, we can feel good about following our own paths, against the expectations imposed upon us by others, and about balancing out our responsibilities with whatever floats our boats.

Hypatia
and
Being a Geek and Proud

(*c.* 370 CE–415 CE)

Aren't libraries the best? Cathedrals for the mind where you can entertain and educate yourself for free, photocopy stuff and rent DVDs from the 1990s. But the Best Library Ever was in Alexandria in Egypt. (Sadly, as with our own illustrious library service, various philistine regimes eventually destroyed it so we can't visit it today.) Founded on the Mediterranean coast in 332 BCE by the Greek celebrity-soldier Alexander the Great, over the centuries Alexandria became the most distinguished centre of learning and enquiry in the ancient world because of its Museum – which was a kind of university – and the aforementioned fabulous library, which is thought to have housed over 500,000 books. The city is also notorious for later being the scene of the romance between its queen, Cleopatra, and Julius Caesar, who conquered it for the Romans in 48 BCE (see Cleopatra on p. 119). Hypatia, its other famous female citizen, was closely associated with the library, but took a rather different approach towards sex and power to that taken by the Queen of the Nile. Nevertheless, in her own way, she also lived the life she wanted without compromise – although, tragically, with a less empowered ending. (Spoiler alert: some guys killed her.)

By 370 CE, when many historians think Hypatia was born, Alexandria had long been a melting pot of different religious and immigrant communities. Given the crappy status of women in the ancient world, it is noteworthy that she grew up to be one of the most famous teachers at the Museum and is now regarded as the first-known significant female mathematician and philosopher. When Hypatia was busy being too school for cool, Alexandria had been part of the divided Eastern Roman Empire for just over eighty years and Christianity was on the up, often causing conflict with the other religious groups in the city. Alexandria was ruled by the Roman Prefect Orestes and the religious leader the Patriarch Cyril, who were in a constant cock-off about who should have the most power.

Hypatia's father also taught at the Museum and decided to invest in her education as if she were a boy. This meant she was given the benefits of academic training and a hearty fitness regime. The loss of her work makes it hard to be accurate about what mathematical advances she was responsible for but she was regarded by contemporaries as a leader in her field. Socrates Scholasticus wrote: 'There was a woman at Alexandria named Hypatia, daughter of the philosopher Theon, who made such attainments in literature and science, as to far surpass all the philosophers of her own time.' Large crowds would visit to hear her lecture and she was an influential figure. This visibility became the source of her downfall – as it often does for women who have gifts and abilities above their station.

One reason Hypatia could punch her way through the glass ceiling was that she never married. Historians believe that, like other earlier classical philosophers, she remained zerogamous to devote her attention to her studies. Celibacy outside the clergy was generally frowned on at this time, so it was a bold move for Hypatia to choose her career over family life. This may have been connected to her admiration of Plato, who didn't believe the idea of the nuclear family was healthy for the state. Stories about her have her down as very beautiful, an excellent public speaker and incontestable smart cookie. Her rejection of the distractions of sex and marriage are illustrated in one legend that says she scared off an admirer by brandishing her used menstrual rag (the equivalent of her bloody tampon) at him: a riot grrrl well before Reading 1992.

Hypatia believed that only she should decide what to do with her bod. Even though the pressure to conform and give it up to boyfriends feels very different nowadays, it is useful to see that there is power to be had in holding on to your hymen (see Elizabeth I on p. 175). We live in a world where sex is everywhere and the female body is still considered public property in many ways, and there is no shame in resisting this and either choosing to avoid the distractions of a sex life or waiting until you're totally convinced the time and person are right.

Hypatia's decisive control of her own body makes the manner of her death particularly horrifying. In 415 CE, Cyril and Orestes' feud went atomic and a mob of Christians, enraged by both Hypatia's influence on Orestes and the non-Christian philosophy she taught, assaulted, kidnapped, stripped, beat and murdered her, apparently with roof tiles. Cyril's predecessor had burned down the last part of the library remaining in the city, and many see Hypatia's death as the nadir of this wave of Christian intolerance towards Ancient Greek learning and civilisation, and the end of this marvellous city's Golden Age. We're lucky that most of us live in places where being a clever woman who speaks out, and doesn't subjugate herself to male authority or sexual desire, is no longer likely to be fatal. Hypatia stands not just as an example of this, but also for all the women who've been told that girls can't do maths, can't read maps and have no spatial awareness: *sambexi* * to that!

* 'Bollocks' in Coptic.

Megan Lloyd George
and
Stepping Out of Your Parents' Shadow

(1902–1966)

History is littered with examples of shady dynasties. From the Khans to the Medicis, the Plantagenets to the Kennedys and the Kims, it's like a messed-up version of *Family Fortunes*, with relatives repeatedly doing one another over in dastardly dynastical power plays. Sometimes a gene pool can get a bit filthy, and it becomes clear it's time to change the water. But it doesn't have to be this way. One generation's success needn't be the following's green light to living it large and disgracing the family name. There's one Welshwoman who wore the mantle of her father's fame beautifully, and managed to make it her own.

Megan Lloyd George was the third daughter, and the fifth and youngest child, of the 'Welsh Wizard' David Lloyd George, who became Prime Minister in 1916 (to date he is the only Welsh-speaking leader this United Kingdom has ever had). Megan was born in the small seaside town of Criccieth, in the shadow of majestic Mount Snowdon. She grew up in Downing Street, initially at number 11, though her patriotic mum insisted that all her sprogs be born in Wales, and they conversed only in *Cymraeg* at home: little Megan was a pure Welsh-speaker until she was four years old. She was home-schooled, partly by Frances Stevenson, her *dadi*'s long-term mistress, whom Megan did not like, not one bit. (DLG and Frances carried on together for thirty years before Megan's mum passed away and they were free to marry, suggesting Frances knew a thing or two about the art of being the other woman. Lloyd George was a well-known lothario, even in what we might think were the pre-sleaze days of Westminster.

Early exposure to political debate sparked Megan's interest in statecraft at a very young age. At the end of World War I, Meg accompanied her dad to the Paris Peace Conference of 1919, at which The Big Three (Prime Minister Lloyd George, Prime Minister Clemenceau of France and President Woodrow Wilson of the US) set out to negotiate a peace 'to end all wars'. They were not *entirely* successful in terms of saving the world from the devastation of another global conflict, but that meeting did set Meg on course for a life of politics.

In 1929, having studied modern history and politics, Megan campaigned for (in Welsh, natch) and won the Anglesey constituency for the Liberals. She took her place with dad and brother Gwylim in the House of Commons, becoming the first female Welsh MP. *Llongyfarchiadau!*[*] A brilliant orator in whichever language she fancied, she remained in politics for the rest of her life.

* Welsh for 'Congratulations!'

She visited Hitler in 1936 with her father: an infamous meeting at which LG Senior praised Hitler as 'the greatest living German'. By all accounts LG Junior was less keen. Seeing international affairs first-hand made her wary of appeasement. She was not the daddy's girl people assumed she would be, and she was the one who advised her father to ask for PM Chamberlain's resignation in 1940, when the tide started to turn against his policy of accommodating Adolf. She was also hot on the idea of a Welsh parliament, which seemed outlandish at the time, but shows how prescient she was. Throughout the forties and fifties her politics drifted to the left, and in 1955 she defected to the Labour Party. In 1957 she fought for the West Wales seat of Carmarthen, which she won, and held until her death from breast cancer at the age of sixty-four.

Away from the political spotlight, Megan had a long illicit romance with fellow politician Philip John Noel-Baker, thrillingly the only man to have won both an Olympic track medal and the Nobel Peace Prize. Less thrillingly, he chucked her when his wife died, presumably suffering from a too-late bout of the guilts. Her private concerns may not have been plain-sailing, but it's clear Megan's major passion was public life. She was famous in her day for all the good stuff: speaking out against Nazism and Spanish fascism, passionately advocating equality for women and parity for her beloved Welsh. Where her father's rep is slightly iffy when it comes to women and his admiration of the worst dictator history has ever recorded, Megan shines as a beacon of progressive popularity. *Diolch yn fawr*,* Ms Lloyd George!

Our parents inevitably exert a powerful influence over our lives, but it's important to make your own way, feeling neither overawed by their achievements, nor hamstrung by their failings. Miscommunication between the generations is inevitable: can the 'rents even begin to imagine how hard it is to juggle Snapchat with Instagram and Twitter whilst monitoring Facebook? Or understand how overwhelming and confusing dating-site acronyms are? What is MW4MW anyway?** For happy adulting, follow Megan's footsteps, respect your elders, be proud of your parents, but most of all, be your own person.

* Welsh for 'Thank you very much'.
** Man and Woman Looking for Man and Woman, of course!

Fe del Mundo
and
Inspiring Sisters

(1911–2011)

Legendary Filipino paediatrician Fe del Mundo managed the miraculous feat of being the first woman to be accepted into Harvard Medical School – at the time a bastion of masculine self-congratulation – more than a decade before they officially agreed to accept women. This is impressive enough, but what she achieved afterwards is even more reason to big up this teeny titan – and it all came about because of her sister.

Fe was born in Manila, the sixth of eight kids. The family was not poverty-stricken – Fe's *ama* was a prominent lawyer – but child mortality rates in the Philippines were high, and three of her siblings died as babies. Having survived the most dangerous years of infancy, it was a harsh blow when her beloved sister Elisa died of peritonitis, an abdominal infection, at the age of eleven. We're going in quite strong and a bit guilt-trippy here, but our first note, if you're in the middle of a familial feud with your sis, is to remember you're lucky to have one in the first place. According to Fe, Elisa had kept a little notebook in which she had recorded her ambition to become a doctor, and Fe decided the least she could do to honour her memory was to aim for the same.

Fe took herself off to the University of the Philippines College of Medicine at the age of fifteen. She specialised in paediatrics, presumably driven by the deaths of her siblings and in the hope that she could try to prevent others having to go through the same ordeal. She graduated as valedictorian and was granted a full scholarship by the President of the Philippines to study at any school she wanted. Smart cookie Fe picked Harvard and they accepted her in 1936 by mistake: bamboozled by the foreign flavour of her name, they failed to realise she was a girl. She later recalled with a smile that she'd been assigned to an all-male dorm. Despite being the only woman on campus, she completed her course, went on to snaffle a Master's at Boston University, and then returned home in 1941, summoned by the government amidst the rumblings of war with Japan.

Japanese troops arrived in Manila early in 1942 and around five thousand Brits, Yanks and other *dayos** were rounded up into internment camps, leaving behind them many vulnerable children. During a sleepless night, Fe came up with the idea of setting up a children's home outside the main camp. Within weeks she had a patient list in the hundreds and a staff of twenty-five hard at work. When the war ended her career bloomed, and in 1948 she became the first woman to head a government general hospital. When

* Tagalog for 'foreigners'.

she grew frustrated by the bullshit of box-ticking governmental bureaucracy (sound familiar?), she fixed on a plan for a dedicated paediatrics centre which she could control herself, and which would offer both preventative and curative medicine for sick kids.

Fe sold every last belonging she had, including her home, to realise her dream, and finally, in 1957, the one-hundred-bed Children's Medical Center was born, followed a few years later by the Institute of Maternal and Child Health. The IMCH is still recognised today as a world leader in paediatric care. Under her aegis huge progress was made in understanding dengue fever, polio and measles, particularly in childhood, and she made leaps and bounds in immunisation programmes, the promotion of breastfeeding and family planning. She also designed a rather nifty bamboo incubator that didn't rely on electricity and was a godsend for parents in rural areas. She was a constant presence in the centre: she made her home on the second floor of the building and never left. Fe was a titch, barely five feet tall in her scrubs, and, despite her willingness to get down and dirty with the sickest of patients, she was fond of a two-tone court shoe and coiffed 'do, even when doing her rounds in a wheelchair in her ninety-ninth year.

Fe's sadness at her sister's wasted promise proved a stimulating spur to achieving great things. And in fact, without getting too happy-clappy about it, we are all sisters – and we can find inspiration from all of womankind. Nothing is sadder than lack of female solidarity. When a female journalist writes a mock-concerned article about a pop star's wrinkly hands, or a 'friend' tells you everyone is saying your new relationship will never last, it's the equivalent of saying 'I don't believe in the sisterhood' – and just like the fairies, a little bit of all of us is extinguished. So let's park the snarkiness, and rein in the nonpliments. Sisters rule. End of.

Sappho
and
Backing Yourself

(*c.* 610 – *c.* 570 BCE)

When it comes to criticism, there ain't nobody nastier than our own sweet self. So how should we go about shushing that belittling inner voice? Original poetess Sappho of Lesbos is there to teach us about accepting ourselves, warts and all.

The Lady of Lesbos was a literary hit in her own time – nine volumes of her works were catalogued at the Library of Alexandria (see Hypatia on p. 55) and the illustrious librarians named her as one of their nine prime poets. She was the only poetess in the Poets' Hall of Fame. Plato, by all accounts a bit of curmudgeon when it came to the virtues of verse, was moved to call her the 'Tenth Muse'.

But by the Middle Ages, almost all Sappho's poems had vanished. Some of that was due to the ravages of time and it didn't help that her specific Aeolic dialect died out. But blame should also lie at the feet of those repressed men who tried to expunge her talent from history. Christian censors were deeply troubled by the joyous sexuality in her poems (one even-handed cleric called her 'a sex-crazed whore who sings of her own wantonness'), and it's said that Pope Gregory VII sent her work to the bonfires. If Sappho had been around to see all this, her confidence might have taken a bit of a knock, but the work has endured, so we can all take heart from that and resolve to hang on in there when the critics are baying.

In the last two decades fragments of *cartonnage* have revealed whole segments of Sappho's rhymes, which had been lost since medieval times. (*Cartonnage* is compressed plaster the Ancient Egyptians and Greeks made from recycled papyrus. It's a bit like finding lost Shakespeare verses on the back of wallpaper.) How did the antiquities experts know that what they'd uncovered was authentic Sappho? Well, large parts of two of her poems did survive, which made these new Sapphic stanzas (a poetic form she is said to have invented) immediately recognisable. You have to be pretty confident to invent a whole new verse style to express your genius properly.

All aspects of her work, her family and her sexuality have been the subject of feverish dissection and speculation. In all honesty, we know very little about her. What we do know is that she has been consistently associated with the liberal island of Lesbos, of which Mytilene – a big hot mess of political drama and rivalries, where the citizens had a reputation for being pretty easy – was the capital. A tenth-century encyclopaedia claimed she was mother to one daughter, a sister to loads of brothers and married to a man named Kerkylas from an island called Andros.

But it's also been pointed out that *kerkos* is slang for penis, and *andros* means man, so this may just be a reworking of a slightly lame ancient joke. We really don't know if she was definitively a lesbian or not, given how profoundly different the Ancients' view of homosexuality was to ours today. Sexuality was far less clearly defined in the seventh century BCE, even in comparison to what we consider our progressive twenty-first-century flexibility – relationships between adult men and pubescent boys were bewilderingly acceptable, and similarly women and teenage girls often had erotic attachments. Five-hundred-odd years after her death, the Roman poet Ovid claimed Sappho ran a kind of romantic finishing school, teaching young girls the art of love, and that she ended her days by leaping off a cliff because of her unrequited pash for a boat-boy called Phaon. The truth is we don't know the truth, and although over many centuries historians have got themselves in a twist over Sappho's straightness or lack thereof, there's no evidence she fretted about this herself in the slightest.

Everything we truly know about Sappho comes from the poetry she left behind. She was deeply in touch with, and open about, her feelings about love. Solon of Athens – one of the great wise men of Greece – asked to be taught one of her verses after hearing it, 'So that

I may learn it and die.' (The ancient equivalent of a five-star review.) She was *that* good. In her famous, yet uninspiringly titled, Fragment 31, she watches jealously as some guy flirts with a girl she's got the hots for. She definitely sounds like a woman with a serious crush. It's a sizzling description of the physical manifestation of desire and how overwhelming love can be – she's all ears a-thrumming and sweaty shaking; symptoms we can recognise if we've ever fallen hard. What's remarkable is how intimate and exposing her words are. The emphasis is on her emotions and how raw they make her feel. Instead of this being a cause for self-loathing, Sappho luxuriates in her weaknesses and fallibilities. She could turn this unflinching gaze to other aspects of her life as well – there's a brilliant poem about ageing in which she bemoans her knackered knees and sagging skin. Yes, she's old, but she is not hiding from it, and in the act of writing about it, she's owning it.

So here are our rules for making sure you have your back, and back yourself. Firstly, you're not perfect and there is nothing wrong with that – in fact, it's a trait you share with all the best people in history. Throughout your life you're bound to come up against other people's judgement – just as Sappho's work did over the centuries – but you should stand strong and try not to sweat the small stuff. And who cares if you like boys or girls or both? You deserve love, and should enjoy it in any form it comes to you. And you should energetically cultivate it for yourself. It doesn't matter what you look like as long as your soul is in good shape. As Sappho herself said: 'For the man who is beautiful is beautiful to see/but the good man will at once beautiful be.'

Emmeline Pankhurst
and
Getting Stuck In

(1858–1928)

We live in deeply unsettling times. When ridiculous men with access to armies and red buttons seem to be in charge all over the place, it feels very tempting to put your fingers in your ears and shout 'La la la la la' to drown out the terrible noise our politicians are making left, right and centre. Tempting, yes, but wrong. Emmeline Pankhurst, champion for the right of women to have a vote in the first place, would have stern (but motivational) words with you.

Born in Moss Side, Manchester, Emmeline Goulden was weaned on the intoxicating milk of radicalism, raised in a family burning with political passion. The eldest of ten children, she is said to have attended her first women's rally at the age of eight, and her forward-thinking parents sent her to a Parisian finishing school in which she was instructed in the arts of book-keeping and chemistry, as well as the usual embroidery and etiquette. In 1879 she married Richard Pankhurst, a barrister twenty-four years older than her and buddy of the great reformer John Stuart Mill. With her husband's support, Ms P. founded the Women's Franchise League – one of their wins was ensuring that married women were able to have a say in local (but not general) elections. This was an early step in the struggle for votes for women – before this, you were lucky if you got a chance to pick the captain of the local knitting club – but still, only those women clever enough to ensnare a husband got their minute at the ballot box.

After Richard's death at the age of sixty-four, Emmeline managed, through the fug of grief, to find solace again in intense social campaigning. She founded the Women's Social and Political Union (WSPU) in 1903 with her three daughters, Christabel, Sylvia and Adela. The Pankhurst gang's goal was simple: votes for women in every election in which men could vote. Frustrated with a lack of progress on this issue across the party spectrum, Emmeline, with her gals at her side, set the political barometer to stormy. Their slogan was 'Deeds, not words', and boy, did they mean it.

The WSPU's dramatic feats included arson attacks, pouring acid into mailboxes, and even (for the *Fifty Shades of Grey* fans among you) attacking Winston Churchill at Bristol Temple Meads rail station with a riding crop. One woman even took her meat cleaver to Velázquez's *Venus* in the National Gallery; she said afterwards that she attacked the most beautiful woman in history as revenge for the government attacking the woman with the most beautiful soul in history – our very own Emmeline. Another, Emily Wilding Davison, ran onto the course at the Epsom Derby in June 1913 and was killed by the King's horse. It's worth noting that these high-stakes stunts were too much for some, and Sylvia and Adela abandoned the WSPU in protest, causing a family rift that never really healed.

When war broke out in 1914, the pragmatic Emmeline called a truce. She recognised that there was a greater cause to fight for – and that there was no point chasing the vote if ultimately there might not be a country in which to cast it. She switched her focus to campaigning for women to join the war effort, and as the boys went to the front to fight for Blighty, women began to take on more traditionally male occupations. Suddenly there were female tram drivers, farmhands and firefighters, and the ladies also took on roles in the civil service, police force and factories. It's no surprise that women began to question why they were being paid less than their male counterparts for identical roles (and it's frankly bonkers, not to mention really boring, that we are having to ask the same question over a hundred years later). Women's rights were back in the spotlight and, in 1918, the Representation of the People Act extended the vote to women over thirty with some stipulations: they had to own property; or be married to a property owner; or be a graduate voting in a university constituency. So not much cop for our younger working-class sisters.

Emmeline died in 1928, agonisingly just two weeks before women finally won the vote on the same terms as their menfolk. Some hair-splitting historians have questioned whether it was Ms Pankhurst's actions or merely the seismic changes of the war that meant that women were finally judged capable of having the vote without frittering it away on fancies. Was it simply that, with so many men dead, it was now impossible for the government to overlook women? In our eyes, Emmeline still deserves our respect, and more importantly we owe it to her to turn up and take part in our democracy – her activism paved the way for a future in which women's equality has never been off the agenda. Yes, politics today is unpredictable and sometimes depressing, but women have a special duty to exercise a right that was so recently fought for and ferociously hard-won. In fact, we'd go so far as suggesting that the next time you have to vote – in a general election, for a staff rep or for the oddest-shaped vegetable at the village show – you make sure you put your best feminist fashion foot forward and array yourself in the WSPU colours of purple, white and green.

Frida Kahlo
and
Finding Your Style

(1907–1954)

Celebrated artist and fashion icon Frida Kahlo had more than her fair share of bad luck. Born near Mexico City, aged six she caught polio which left her with a limp, and as a student she was caught up in a horrific bus crash, and broke her pelvis and spine when she was impaled by a metal handrail. She faced repeated gruelling operations for the remainder of her life. However, she transmuted her misfortune into fierce art that still has the power to move us today.

Frida was blessed with a father who respected her and galvanised her to look beyond the stereotypical feminine virtues. He championed her education and even encouraged her to take up wrestling to help with her recovery. She began painting while bedbound, and she also started to replicate the bold, rich palette of her works in her clothing. Her fashion-forward choices set her apart from the sober and neat 1930s silhouettes of European and American fashions. Instead she embraced traditional Mexican embroidered blouses, corsets, wide ruffled skirts and a lot of popping colour. She made a point of wearing clothes from the matriarchal society of Tehuantepec in southern Mexico, where the women wield economic power and take no shit. The wide skirts she designed for herself covered her damaged legs and the corsets were like the plaster casts she had to wear after her operations (which she also painted and decorated richly: one with a cheeky hammer-and-sickle icon).

Her self-portraits exhibit her stunning wardrobe and her famous facial hair: she was said by some to purposefully darken her monobrow and 'tache, which she celebrated in opposition to the ideals of glabrous feminine beauty. As you can tell, Frida was an unconventional and political person in every aspect of her life – as well as being fantastically glamorous and stylish. She was a committed member of the Mexican Communist Party (taking that commitment as far as banging Trotsky when he was living in Mexico). Fashion may seem like the least profound element in her career but it is deeply entwined with her other concerns – her sympathy with the oppressed, her belief in the connections between all people and her efforts to celebrate the female experience in all its visceral glory – and is part of her enduring legacy. She *was* her art.

Frida's love life was also gloriously colourful. She married the famous painter Diego Rivera when she was twenty-two and he was forty-three. They supported each other in their work but they lived in separate houses. She referred to him as the 'other accident'. As her work developed, she explored the most intimate and difficult parts of her life in her paintings – from her operations to her abortions and miscarriages. The link between her physical, emotional and artistic lives was extremely strong and she also expressed this sartorially: when Diego had an affair with her sister, she cut off all her long dark hair, which she often wore in braids adorned with flowers, as a sign of her distress (a classic break-up haircut). The couple divorced but then remarried each other in 1940, two years after Frida's first big solo show in New York. She went on to become the first Latin American woman to be exhibited in the Louvre. André Breton referred obliquely to her style when he called her art 'a ribbon around a bomb'.

Not long after Frida's first solo exhibition in Mexico in 1953, which she attended in her bed, she had her right leg amputated. She designed her own fancy prosthetic leg featuring a decorated red platform boot with a bell, again transforming her injuries into material for her creativity. She used her clothes to make herself feel stronger on days when she was in pain, as well as to assert her identity as part of the top celeb art couple of the time. Ill health finally got the better of the fabulous Ms Kahlo in 1954 and she died, far too young, aged just forty-seven. On her death, Diego locked her wardrobe and asked for its contents to remain hidden for fifty years, showing how significant her clothes were to her life. The closet's contents were finally revealed in 2004 when photographs went on display in the Frida Kahlo museum in Mexico City.

Frida is an outstanding illustration of a woman creating her own persona through her fashion choices, which were both political and practical. Her clothes allowed her to display her exuberance and wit, her identification with the working class of her country and its traditions, and expressed her unique concept of beauty. You don't need to be defined by the hypersexualised celebrity standards of attractiveness that bombard us relentlessly. You have the means to choose how and why you decorate yourself: to create your own style, to reflect your unique personality, to act as both armour and advert for yourself, and just for the sheer joy of dressing up.

Ada Lovelace
and
Surviving a Broken Home

(1815–1852)

If there's one thing worse than a broken home, it's a broken celebrity home. Glamorous, gallivanting George Gordon, Lord Byron, famously failed to keep it in his britches. It's always incredibly painful when a parent abandons the family, but so much worse when you become the object of gossip and pity. Byron's mathematician daughter, Ada Lovelace, managed to pull off intellectual triumph over emotional chaos. She did not let her father's clichéd behaviour hold her back. Ada is now widely celebrated as the author of the world's first published algorithm and one of the first people to conceive of what modern computers might do. But her parents' separation cast a long shadow over her childhood, which Ada had to work hard to escape – both in forging her own path without her father's assistance and in battling with the bad precedent he set.

Ada didn't lay eyes on her illustrious pater from the day he decamped when she was just five weeks old. Her spurned mother kept his portrait covered with a thick curtain. (There was clearly a penchant for a touch of drama in the Byron household.) But Ada's mother was not one to channel her rage solely into theatrical soft furnishings: she had been well educated and encouraged her daughter to study science in an attempt to prevent her from growing up to become a loose-knickered poet like her dad. She engaged top tutors for her daughter, even though universities were not open to women at the time.

Ada met Charles Babbage, superbrain and 'father of the computer', when she was seventeen and they corresponded fruitfully about his ambitious plans to invent a steam-powered calculating machine, and later his pioneering Analytical Engine. Ada was twenty-seven when she published the definitive paper on the Analytical Engine, the significance of which went uncelebrated (the ladies of history raise their eyebrows and sigh with recognition at this point) until good old ~~Benedict Cumb~~ . . . Alan Turing brought it to public attention in the 1950s. Despite repeated ill health – leading to her addiction to opium – the asthmatic Ada worked day and night on her studies. If she could overcome a dick of a dad, an intense mother, a patriarchal society and a serious illness, and still climb to greatness and contribute to the future, then you certainly can too.

In the interests of full disclosure, a dedication to science didn't entirely make Ada a dull and disciplined young lady. Doubt was cast on her fidelity to her husband and she used her mathematical prowess to invent a system to help her win at her favourite hobby of gambling (unsuccessfully). Undoubtedly an original, ahead of her time, Ada now has a day in October dedicated to her and the celebration of all women in science – an opportunity to sink a laudanum tonic and play a round of poker in her honour.

Mekatilili wa Menza
and
Finding your Rhythm

(c. 1860s – c. 1925)

Hands in the air. A rush of goodwill towards your fellow ravers. When you're properly feeling it, dancing is one of the great free joys in life. The liberation we feel is typical of dancers across the ages. From the highly stylised courtly dances of the Renaissance to the passionate tangos of Argentina (which were banned in the 1980s by officials for having 'other meanings') the dancefloor has been a space where women in particular have long been able to express themselves. As far as we can tell, rebel leader Mekatilili wa Menza was the first to use dance, not exactly as a weapon, but certainly as an instrument of resistance.

Mekatilili was a member of the Giriama tribe in what is now eastern Kenya; the only daughter in a poverty-stricken family of five siblings. Little is known of her early childhood, though one incident might give an insight into her political stance in later life – as a young girl she witnessed one of her brothers being snatched by Arab slavers at a market. Historians believe it was this traumatic event that activated her highly sensitive radar to the whiff of oppression.

In the late nineteenth century, missionary-cum-explorer David Livingstone had announced that he believed the only way to stamp out the slave trade was to introduce the three Cs – commerce, Christianity and civilisation – to Africa. The 'commerce' bit of this was obviously the most popular – there was a helluva lot of gold to be had – and so began the 'Scramble for Africa' in which esurient European powers, notably Britain, France, Portugal and Germany, colonised vast swathes of the continent. The British took control of Kenya from 1895. By 1913, the colonials were not only trying to use the Giriama men for cheap labour, but also making noises about recruiting them into the army to fight for the British in the looming war against the Germans. Mekatilili, now in her fifties, wasn't having it. Appalled by the idea that her fellow tribesmen were being pushed to risk their lives in a war that wasn't theirs, she vehemently and vocally opposed British officials: at one meeting she was said to have gone as far as giving the local administrator a good slap. As a woman, Mekatilili would not usually have been permitted to pipe up, but in Giriama culture widows are allowed to speak even before elders, and she took full advantage of the privileges accorded to her.

Mckatilili made her opinion clear on issues such as over-taxation, conscription and the erosion of traditional tribal religion and culture. But how did a middle-aged woman of no significant standing get people to pay attention? She danced her ass off, that's how. As a fervent practitioner of tribal ritual, she was well aware of the power of one particular dance – the *kifudu*. The *kifudu* is usually performed at funerals. A female dancer, accompanied by male musicians, dances it to bring communities together and celebrate the ancestors at the moment of their departure. Mekatilili danced it from village to village like a whirling Pied Piper of Hamelin, whipping up the crowds, and then giving extraordinary rallies and speeches lamenting the bloody British and how they were sending her country to the dogs. She was by all accounts a natural leader and an extremely charismatic person and the spectacular effect she produced was testament to both her physical and verbal eloquence.

The support Mekatilili roused led to the Giriama Uprising, which spooked the Brits. They arrested this most inspiring of political choreographers in October 1913, with her co-rebel, resistance leader Wanje wa Mwadorikola. Both were deported across the continent so they could be locked up away from their community. But the dynamic duo escaped and trekked the thousand kilometres back home to keep on fighting the fight, apparently falling in love along the way. The British couldn't understand how they hadn't died en route and, instead of recognising her grit, suspected her of having supernatural powers. For the Giriama this only cemented her reputation as a prophetess of prodigious proportions. Mekatilili was arrested again and this time sent to the Somali border, but managed to ghost once again and carried on with her agitating.

By 1919 the British were so stretched by their efforts in World War I that they caved, and many of the powers stripped from the tribe were returned. Scant evidence exists, but it seems that Mekatilili was installed as leader of the women's council of elders and Wanje became head the of the men's council. Mekatilili died in around 1925. We like to think she kept dancing right up to the end.

This grandmother of groove shows that there are many ways to campaign for what you believe in. Everyone can turn their unique talents to a cause. Dance is one of the most vital and dynamic of the ways humans express themselves: your hips don't lie and nothing quite lifts the spirits like a riotous rave. So kick off your shoes, roll out your robot, vamp up your vogue, master your moonwalk and dance like *everyone* is watching.

Wang Zhenyi
and
Slamming it as a Scientista

(1768–1797)

M any of the ladies in this book would have chor- tled into their fichus if you had told them that paralysed limbs could be reanimated thanks to cyber- netic implants in the brain. Or that we would locate and identify oxygen in a galaxy 13.2 billion light years away. But before we get all back-patty about our leaps and bounds in the progress of human endeav- our, it is worth remembering that the world of science can seem extraordinarily backwards when it comes to those with two X chromosomes.

A recent study showed that women make up just 12.8 per cent of the STEM (Science, Technology, Engineering and Maths) workforce. The words of a Nobel Prize-winning biochemist weren't all that encouraging either – he said three things happen when women are in the lab: 'you fall in love with them, they fall in love with you and when you criti- cise them, they cry'.

Aside from dealing with the odd misogynist, the scientific world offers any girl a future bright with opportunity. Just try not to look too distractingly sexy in your lab coat, OK? Who wouldn't fancy navigating NASA's rover over the terrain of Mars? Or becoming a flavourist, dreaming up new smells and tastes to get the palate turned on? Or a conservationist, working with governments to find ways to protect our planet?

We humans are hard-wired to be curious about the mysteries of the world around us but it's also true that it can sometimes be drummed out of us in tedious, formulaic school lessons.

Wang Zhenyi, the Brian Cox of eighteenth-century China, was a woman who understood the importance of maths and science in a person's education. She genuinely loved her subjects and realised that the key to learning was accessibility. Originally taught by her grandparents and her father, she was lucky enough to grow up in a household full of books. She was a dazzling polymath – as well as mistressing maths and astronomy, she wrote poetry, and was an excellent equestrian and martial artist. And she did all this in a time when feudal customs made life as a woman very restrictive. Women were considered morally, emotionally and intellectually inferior, and small feet were prized over huge minds (see Empress Dowager Cixi on p. 241).

Wang was a fan of a text called *The Principles of Calculation* by the eminent (male) mathematician Mei Wending. It was written in aristocratic, rather impenetrable language so she rewrote it as *The Simple Principles of Calculation* in a clear and easy-to-follow style. A bit like a *Dummies* guide. She did the same thing in volumes on the Pythagorean theorem and trigonometry. It wasn't easy: 'There were times I had

103

to put down my pen and sigh. But I love the subject. I do not give up,' she wrote.

She was also an avid experimenter. Her 'Explanation of a Lunar Eclipse' – a fun and straightforward visual explanation of a complex astronomical event – is considered pretty accurate even today. It's worth remembering she was living in a time when it was thought that lunar eclipses were a sign of the gods' anger. Most people had probably realised there wasn't really a great dragon rising up to spread darkness, but still, folk reckoned it was bad juju. Not Ms Zhenyi. 'Actually,' she wrote, 'it's definitely because of the moon.' And she proceeded to demonstrate this in a famous physical experiment where she set up a round table in a garden pavilion to represent the earth, with a lamp hanging from the rafters of the pavilion as the sun, and a round mirror for the moon. By mimicking the conditions of an eclipse, she showed that they occur when the moon passes into the earth's shadow, rather than when a crazed god gets in a snit.

Wang's poetry was also impressive. It was stripped back and direct, rather than the flowery stuff that was associated with female poets at the time. Her subjects and themes were unusual too; she penned this, about gender equality:

It's made to believe,
Women are the same as Men;
Are you not convinced,
Daughters can also be heroic?

Wang died startlingly young from illness, at the age of twenty-nine. She was an academic ace whose incandescent precocity was extinguished far too soon. She understood that science can be mesmerising, mindboggling and mysterious – you just need to see the beauty in it. And she wasn't up for being pigeon-holed as a sciencey or artsy person – she showed you can be both. So dust off your lab coats, women, engage your neural pathways, and say hello to a career as a marine biologist in the Maldives, or a sound engineer rocking it in Vegas. You never know, you might end up with a Venusian crater named after you, just like Wang Zhenyi.

Emily Dickinson
and
Defying FOMO

(1830–1886)

Your frenemy is in an annoyingly cute floral head-dress and posting sun-drenched festival pics on IG; your best friend is humblebragging about how 'feisty' her gorgeous baby is on Facebook; your cousin is doing impossible yoga poses in expensive sports-wear on a beach. At sunset. In St Lucia . . . You are in your flat taking a rest from eating pot noodles in front of Netflix and cleaning out the mouse shit from under the sofa. Venturing onto social media can sometimes feel like having a thousand turmeric lattes thrown in your face. Everyone everywhere else seems to be having such a fabulous time – #seizetheday #yolo #treat-yoself – so it's no surprise that we all occasionally suf-fer from fear of missing out. But do you really want to live an Instalife? FOMO can lead you to do things you don't actually care about and swiftly suck you into a whirlwind of triviality. Perhaps we should choose where we invest our time more carefully, and start not giving a fig about where everyone else is going? Iconic poet and recluse Emily Dickinson was not immune to social angst: she worried a lot about her friendships, and frequently wrote about loneliness in her work, but she never let social convention and the expectations of the crowd lead her anywhere she didn't want to go. Now she's considered one of the most original voices the English language has ever produced. That mofo

FOMO can have destructive effects on psychological well-being so it's worth learning from the exceptional Em D.

Emily was born in Amherst, Massachusetts. This was a good place to be a nineteenth-century girl as it was easier for women to access education there than in other parts of the US. Em was a sociable lass and close to her siblings: she lived with her sister Vinnie all her life and her brother and his family were just next door. Her brother married one of Emily's closest friends, Susan, a clever, curious and cultivated woman who became something of an intellectual mentor to her (see Althea Gibson on p. 169) and with whom she corresponded and shared her poetry for years. They also bonded over a frustration with all the womanly chores they had to put up with.

Emily wasn't the sort of poet to bloviate loudly about her genius at every opportunity: she only published a few poems in her lifetime and her family didn't find her manuscript books of 1,800 poems until after her death. She was a master pen pal: she used letters to connect with people she cared about, and was interested in intellectually, and to learn more about the world. In her early twenties Emily gradually removed herself from the f2f world. She learned the magical art – which many women lack – of saying no.

Several reasons for her hermitage have been mooted: from the idea that she was busy running the household with Vinnie while her mother was sick, to the speculation that she had been depressed by the deaths of several people close to her and the turbulence of the American Civil War. Over time she appeared to grow more eccentric, insisting on wearing only white dresses (a supercool look but one that must've required a lot of laundry), but she was also, unknown to most, concentrating on her poetry. When the rest of her family joined the Amherst Congregational Church, Emily did not. She was not afraid of going her own way. After the death of her beloved eight-year-old nephew Gilbert, she stopped leaving the house at all, writing to one of her male friends who had asked her to visit: 'I do not cross my Father's ground to any House or town.'

Emily's poetry is stylistically unique, lyrical, profound and often concerned with death and love. Just as she defied social expectations, so her poems defied literary convention:

> Tell all the truth but tell it slant —
> Success in Circuit lies . . .

Their enigmatic quality has led to lots of speculation about her love life:

Wild nights – Wild nights!
Were I with thee
Wild nights should be
Our luxury!

We know that she corresponded affectionately with various men and women and that in her later life she had a romantic relationship with an older widowed friend of her father's, Otis Phillips Lord, until his death in 1884. Emily herself died at the age of fifty-five in 1886, her coffin filled with flowers from her beloved garden.

Emily resisted FOMO to concentrate on her art, which she didn't create to show off, but for her own personal fulfilment. In our attention-grabbing superficial world there is surely something to be said for that. She is also a good reminder of the joys of having your own bedroom, the place where she wrote most, and which she told her niece gave her the greatest freedom. So next time you're looking at glamorous holiday pics, or hilarious party snaps on your friends' timelines, log off, go to your room, and celebrate some quality unplugged time with yourself, Belle of Amherst style.

Phoolan Devi

and

Not Being a Lady

(1963–2001)

If we call a bloke a gentleman we are implying that they are a morally upstanding person, as well as handy with their ps and qs. Being 'ladylike' exudes a perfumed aura of gentility, wafting elegance and polished femininity. 'Lady' attributes seem unlikely to help you win in a dog-eat-dog world, where being demure can make you look like a pushover. However, it is possible to be both feminine and firm: you can wear nice skirts and be kind while you ascend to the top, and politely make crystal clear what you will or won't accept from other people. Equally, there is no reason that being judged as 'unladylike' should muzzle your magnificence if you have more of a plain-speaking, tomboy thing going on.

Bandit Queen turned politician Phoolan Devi was *not* a lady, not by any measure. There is no definitive version of her life story but it is generally agreed that she was born into a low-caste family in Uttar Pradesh in India. Even at ten years old, she was famously sweary and flexed her mettle when she argued with her older cousin in a dispute over a family plot of land. Her delightful cuz responded by smacking her in the head with a brick and persuading her parents to marry her off to a man in his thirties from a different village. Early life for Phoolan was a very literal school of hard knocks.

Phoolan's new husband was brutal and abusive and she absconded back home. Naturally, she was henceforth considered a slut by her village. In 1979 she rowed with her cousin again and this time he had her thrown in jail: an exceptionally unpleasant place for a teenage girl. The same year she either ran away or was kidnapped by a violent criminal gang, who hung out in the rural Chambal Valley robbing trucks and landowners and getting themselves a bit of a Robin Hood rep. The high-caste leader of the crew was killed by his deputy Vikram when he tried to assault Phoolan. Vikram then took over the operation, with Phoolan by his side. He taught her to shoot and she ran with the gang, including paying her ex-husband a visit to beat him up in retaliation for his violence towards her when she was his child bride.

In 1980, things went disastrously wrong for Phoolan when two former high-caste gang members were released from prison, murdered Vikram and took charge. They raped Phoolan and imprisoned her in a hut for three weeks in the village of Behmai. Another gang member eventually helped her escape and she set up a splinter group, gaining a reputation as the fearsome Bandit Queen.

Phoolan was not one to let the violence and disrespect she endured in Behmai go unanswered.

Prefiguring Arya Stark, she said: 'Once I became a *dacoit* (bandit) and started making lists of all the people who had tortured me, who had abused me, and I was able to pay them back in kind, that pleased me tremendously.' In February 1981 she returned to Behmai with her squad, initially disguised as police officers. They gathered the villagers. Referring to the men who killed Vikram and assaulted her, Phoolan said: 'I know that [they] are hiding in this village. If you don't hand them over to me, I will stick my gun in your butts.' When no one stepped forward, the upper-caste men – twenty-two in all – were murdered. Whether or not Phoolan was present or fully responsible for the killing is unclear. It became known as the St Valentine's Day Massacre and cemented in folklore this young, five feet tall, low-caste woman in her bandana and khakis as a dangerous and terrifying criminal.

After two years on the run, Phoolan surrendered, in return for immunity from the death penalty for her and her followers. She staged her capitulation in front of pictures of Gandhi and the warrior goddess Durga. She was charged with forty-eight crimes but was kept in prison without trial for eleven years until her controversial pardon in 1994. While she was in jail her health failed and she was operated on, leading to a hysterectomy. Allegedly the surgeon commented: 'We don't want her breeding any more Phoolan Devis.' In the same year as her pardon, a film of her life, *Bandit Queen*, based on a 1991 biography, was released. Despite the film's heroic portrayal of her, Phoolan hated the way she was pictured as a victim rather than a resilient leader.

After serving her time, Phoolan turned her irrepressible energy towards a better cause. She married a politician and just two years after leaving prison, despite being illiterate and innumerate, she successfully ran for office, campaigning for the rights of the poor and women. However, just five years later, this thirty-something woman who had most definitely lived by the sword, died by the sword. She was assassinated outside her home by an upper-caste man avenging the St Valentine's Day Massacre.

So what does this mistreated, violent, contentious figure have to teach us? Phoolan is celebrated as one of the most heroic, and vilified as one of the most evil, women in history. As a role model, she is definitely problematic. Murder is clearly not an acceptable answer to anything, but in the society Phoolan inhabited violence towards women was depressingly par for the course and it was unusual for them to retaliate. After imprisonment Phoolan turned her forceful nature and fearless ability to confront difficulty to more positive ends in her political career. Her fantastic swearing is also to be much admired; nothing beats a good curse in the right circumstances – refinement be damned. When an interviewer asked whether the profanity indulged in by her character in the film was accurate she replied: 'Oh, that's totally wrong. In real life I swear a lot more.' She may not have been a lady, but man, was she all woman.

Cleopatra
and
Keeping Your Family in Line

(c. 69–30 BCE)

No one knows just what buttons to press as much as your brother or sister does. It's an intense relationship, and things can go really, really wrong when we vie for our parents' attention. Who among us has not tried to convince a sibling that they were in fact purchased from the supermarket, or taken a pair of scissors to their favourite doll's hair because, well, just because? But there's a cautionary tale from history for those who push their nearest and dearest too far, as demonstrated by the one and only Queen of the Nile. As well as being famed for her staggering political power plays, passionate love affairs and spectacular charisma, Cleopatra – or Cleopatra VII Thea Philopator, to give her full, impressive title – knew a thing or two about family dynamics, and nowhere did she demonstrate it more ruthlessly than in her brutal ascent to power.

Cleopatra ruled jointly with her father, Ptolemy XII Auletes, until his death when she was eighteen. According to Egyptian custom she could not stay on the throne without a male consort, so she was married off to her twelve-year-old brother, Ptolemy XIII, which was not at all creepy in the Egypt of the time. There was no question as to who was in charge, though, and over time canny Cleo had her brother's name all but erased from official documents. Cleopatra understood the power of a sharp brain, the impact of a grand gesture, and she scored highly on what we would now call emotional intelligence. She had an incredible speaking voice (many believe it was this, rather than her physical beauty, that made her so seductive) and she was fluent in twelve languages, which meant that she could dispense with translators, diplomats and, indeed, advisors when dealing with foreign potentates. She often made big decisions without even consulting her court. Her chief advisor and one of her generals couldn't handle that level of bossness and sneakily conspired to overthrow Cleopatra and send her into exile. They replaced her with her more malleable little brother.

Meanwhile, in Greece, Julius Caesar was on the ascent, having triumphed over his rival Pompey the Great, who also happened to be Cleopatra and her siblings' guardian. Pompey sought refuge in Egypt, but was murdered by the now teenage Ptolemy XIII and his entourage. This move was meant to secure Caesar's favour but infuriated him instead: he was still loyal to his fellow Roman and former son-in-law, and if anyone was going to be the dispenser of justice it would be JC himself, not some power-crazed pubescent. So he travelled to Egypt and installed himself in the Royal Palace. Cleopatra, watching from afar, sensed her opportunity to regain her position, and had herself delivered to Caesar rolled up in a rug, as you do. The mighty general was instantly bewitched, and by the time her brother arrived the following morning to negotiate, Cleopatra and Caesar had already hooked up. In the war that followed, Ptolemy XIII drowned in the Nile and Arsinoe, the sister who sided with him and declared herself Queen at Cleopatra's palace, was exiled to the Temple of Artemis at Ephesus. Cleopatra persuaded her new beau, Mark Antony, to have Arsinoe killed some years later, proving the old adage that absolutely no one can screw you over quite like your own family.

OK, Cleopatra's actions are a little drastic if you're trying to figure out how to trump your sibling (and we'd prefer you channelled Fe del Mundo's sororal affection, p. 67). However, in the midst of a feud of any kind there is something to be learned from her audacity and single-mindedness, her understanding that knowledge is power, her self-reliance, and her willingness to employ a bit of theatre to get noticed. Should you need to go nuclear at any point, she provides an interesting strategy for coming out on top. Hail Cleopatra: that 'Rare Egyptian', as Shakespeare saw it, who 'beggar'd all description'.

Dorothy Parker
and
Handling Jerks

(1893–1967)

It is a truth universally acknowledged that, at the exact moment you fully invest in a relationship, the object of your affections turns out to be an emotionally immature sociopath.

Experience tells us that there is no point attempting to change your beloved jerk's behaviour if you make this distressing diagnosis. But just think of the material it gives you for bitching with your friends, moaning to your mother and penning vengeful WhatsApp messages to your crew. And there's one spiky sister from history who took her painful romantic experiences and transformed them into the most cracking copy. Dorothy Parker was a literary alchemist who turned her dejection into professional comedy gold. No one remembers her husbands or the names of her negligent paramours – but her words are etched onto our psyches as the best retorts ever committed to paper. How could one possibly better 'It serves me right for putting all my eggs in one bastard' (about the man who knocked her up, resulting in an abortion), 'Take me or leave me; or, as is the usual order of things, both', or 'Ducking for apples – change one letter and it's the story of my life.'

Dorothy Rothschild was the fourth child of a moderately prosperous couple who lived happily in Manhattan until Dorothy's mother died. Her father remarried a devout Catholic whom Dotty did not take to, refusing to address her as Mother, Stepmother or even her given name, preferring instead 'the housekeeper'. Ouch. Dot had a keen eye for turning personal tragedy into great stories, so it's hard to know how much of her family myth is just that, but we do know that in 1917 she married Edwin Pond Parker II, a quietly alcoholic stockbroker. The marriage was unhappy, and it's said she had several affairs, notably with the writer Charles MacArthur (he of the eggs and bastard). She also began to throw herself into work.

In 1918 Dorothy became the theatre critic of *Vanity Fair*, replacing none other than P. G. Wodehouse, and she quickly developed a reputation as one of the most vicious voices in journalism. She was a regular at the daily lunch of the infamous 'Algonquin Round Table', where the most loquacious scribblers, actors and wits of the day would meet to verbally scrap it out. In 1920 she was fired and went freelance, publishing poems and stories, and in 1927 landed a gig as a book reviewer for *The New Yorker*. She would be its 'Constant Reader' until the end of her life.

Dorothy lived at a time when the hedonism of the 1920s was revolutionising life for middle-class women: they cut their hair short, smoked, drank, embraced the sexual revolution, took pride in backchat, drove cars, indulged in consumerism and listened to jazz. The respectable older generation viewed them as a dangerous, reckless force for evil. There was also plenty of handwringing from old-school feminists who had campaigned for political equality and questioned the flappers' self-absorption and wondered if the pursuit of having-it-all would in fact result in having-not-very-much – and a life that felt lonely, disappointed and bitter. Sound familiar, O woman of the twenty-first century? For Parker, though, the freedom to write the human condition – painful, heart-breaking, but often very, very funny – was paramount.

Her marriage to Edwin ended in divorce in the late 1920s, and in 1932 Parker met Alan Campbell, a much younger actor who had published a few short stories. They married in 1934, and soon after were approached by an agent who told them they could make it big in Hollywood, baby, and they did indeed become successful scriptwriters, even being nominated for two Academy Awards. In LA, Dorothy became a political activist; she opposed the rise of fascism in Germany and Spain, and was investigated by the FBI. Her second marriage failed but her activism endured, and on her death she left everything in her will to Dr Martin Luther King Jr, with her estate eventually going to the NAACP (see Rosa Parks on p. 25).

She had written her own epitaph, 'Excuse my dust', yet another masterclass in devastating brevity, but in a strange twist concerning an argument over her will, the urn containing her ashes languished in her attorney's filing cabinet for seventeen years, until the NAACP insisted it be interred at their HQ in Baltimore.

So the next time you get ghosted after the third date, or find yourself baffled by the fact that your partner is incapable of expressing emotion, think of Dorothy Parker and her exceptional, unforgettable ability to turn even the most embarrassing romantic rejection into a pithy, polished putdown. Yes, there's despair in her writing about the misery of a woman's lot, but her defiance, vicious wit and superhuman cocktail-swilling capacity for partying shines through. She was the enemy of the boring and mundane, a sister of sass with a razor-sharp mind.

Fanny Cochrane Smith
and
Finding Your Own Voice

(1834–1905)

Nothing is more frustrating than obnoxious behaviour in the meeting room. There's the person who cannot sit through a half-hour discussion without fiddling with their phone, the guy who makes a 'hurry up' motion with his hand whenever someone else is talking, and our least favourite: the circular conversation where each person paraphrases the last and jack shit gets done. One of the most common complaints of women in the workplace is the difficulty of making themselves heard, and research shows that even if one does make herself heard she will be considered less competent than her male counterpart. Fanny Cochrane Smith, the very last speaker of indigenous Tasmanian, understood the importance of finding, and keeping, your own voice. Her story offers us a lesson in overcoming the worst life has to throw at you, and staying true to who you are, even when others are trying to shut you down.

When European explorers first came to Tasmania in 1803, the Aboriginal population numbered around four thousand souls. One hundred years after the British contingent got their infamously insensitive hands on the island, they had all but vanished. From the off, relations between the settlers and islanders were dreadful; the colonisers' approach was barbarous – rape and murder being popular pastimes. By 1830, the Black War had practically decimated the Aboriginal Tasmanians and someone had the brilliant idea that segregation would be the magic answer to the conflict. In 1834, 134 Aborigines were 'persuaded' to relocate to Flinders Island for the chilling process of being 'civilised and Christianised'. Flinders was grim – the weather was terrible and crops wouldn't grow. Cut off from their culture and home, many died of a lethal combination of physical and mental misery.

Fanny Cochrane was one of the first children born on Flinders, to a mother inauspiciously named Tanganutura, which means 'to weep bitterly'. Fanny's name was given to her by her 'civilisers' on Flinders, another example of the assault on Aboriginal culture. At seven, Fanny was sent back to the mainland, ostensibly to learn domestic skills but in fact to live in an orphanage resembling a brutal prison – think *Oliver Twist* with added violence. At the age of twelve, she returned to the island to work in the home of the prison catechist, a classic overseer baddie who treated her appallingly and often kept her in chains. She, pleasingly, tried to burn his house down.

By 1847 it was clear that the Flinders project had failed, and the forty-seven survivors, including Fanny, were moved back to the mainland. There she married William Smith, an English ex-convict whose donkey-stealing proclivities had resulted in his transportation. Together they built an impressive life. They had eleven children, ran a boarding house and made their income from timber. Fanny was famous for her cooking and her strength; she regularly walked the fifty kilometres into Hobart for supplies. But in creating a good life for herself and her family, Fanny didn't turn her back on her oppressed community. She converted to Methodism but refused to sever her close ties with her people, revelling in bush craft, traditional customs and songs. In 1876, Fanny took up the claim to be the last Aboriginal solely of Tasmanian descent recognised by the Tasmanian parliament in 1889. Just imagine how weird it would be to know you were the last person on the planet to know your culture's tongue, stories and songs. Instead of disappearing down a wormhole of existential rage and loneliness, Fanny decided to travel across her land making sure she and the language of her people were heard.

It was at one of her recitals that she came across Horace Watson, a wealthy entrepreneur and early marketing guru. He realised the historical import of Fanny and her status as the last gatekeeper of a language on the verge of extinction, and decided to make phonograph recordings of her speaking and singing, which we can still listen to today. Fanny died in 1905 but nearly a century later the community of Tasmanian Aboriginals, including Fanny's descendants, decided to reconstruct the indigenous language. By 2013, enough words had been recovered to produce a dictionary – no mean feat for an almost entirely oral language.

Fanny Cochrane Smith literally and metaphorically found her own voice; she was a bridge between two cultures that still stands today. There is something extraordinarily moving about her scratchy, warbling recordings – full of defiance and joy. By pushing herself forward and speaking out, she has left us a priceless cultural legacy.

Marie Stopes
and
Not (necessarily) Having Babies

(1880–1958)

You would think that the conversation about a woman's right to choose what happens to her body would be over by now. 'I can't believe we're still protesting this shit' was a regular placard spotted at the women's marches in 2017. But sadly, when that unqualified guy signs an executive order on his very first day in office removing funding for groups that provide information about abortion, we know we can't sit back and rest on our ovaries just yet. A recent study showed 44 per cent of pregnancies around the world were unintended. Pregnancy and birth are huge physical and psychological deals, let alone the lifetime rearing children thereafter. Many feminists consider the ability to decide whether or not to undertake them as the single most liberating thing to have happened to women in history.

So it's worth casting our minds back to one of the women who made this possible. Family planning pioneer Dr Marie Stopes was born in Edinburgh to a suffragist mum and an archaeologist dad. Her first career sounds mint – she was a fossil-hunting palaeobotanist, graduating with a first from University College London, sprinkling on a PhD from Munich University and topping it all off by becoming the first female academic at Manchester University. They offered her the post by mistake, but felt they couldn't withdraw it (insert nudge-nudge, wink-wink here). Her first marriage, to fellow scientist Reginald Ruggles Gates, was a flop (it's just too easy) after she discovered he was impotent, and their union was quickly annulled.

As well as being an expert in the sex lives of flowers, Stopes was also interested in her own, and took a scientific approach to it. Her biographer talks of a record she kept whilst doing a bit of solo camping after her divorce called 'Tabulation of Symptoms of Sexual Excitement in Solitude', which sounds much more rewarding than bullet journalling. It's thought she also had a passionate affair with a Japanese professor on her travels. She turned her experience of sexual frustration in her marriage into a revolutionary sex manual aimed at women and scoffed at the idea that it was improper for a woman to enjoy nookie (in those days it was seen as more ladylike for wives to lie back and think of England rather than have any fun). The book, entitled *Married Love*, brought her huge fame and the blazing wrath of the Catholic Church, which only intensified when she followed it up with another runaway bestseller, *Wise Parenthood*, which was a concise guide to contraception. She married Humphrey Verdon Roe, who shared her interest in birth control, the following year.

But it was in Marie's clinics that the really trail-blazing work took place. She opened The Mothers' Clinic in London in 1921; a truly ground-breaking place where female doctors dispensed free advice and contraceptives to women who wanted to choose whether to have another mouth to feed or not. Though this seems incontrovertibly sensible, many were outraged. The Catholic writer Dr Halliday Sutherland wrote a book in which he implied that Marie was sweet-talking Germans (a dangerous accusation in the post-World War I years) and experimenting on the poor, and that some of her work was illegal. She took him to court for libel and there was long back and forth, appeal and counter-appeal, with some pretty dubious judging thrown in for good measure. Marie ended up losing, but the air-time given to her views was something money couldn't buy. Through the 1920s she opened more clinics, and in 1930 created the National Birth Control Council, which still thrives today as the Family Planning Association, helping millions of people take their sexual and reproductive health into their own hands.

Marie herself was a big personality, prone to self-aggrandisement and some frankly disturbing views which we shouldn't gloss over. She was a true radical, but that radicalism extended to some pretty out-there stuff. For example, her nastiest belief was encouraging sterilisation, particularly for the poor. And she was a racist, believing southern Italians to be a 'lower' race, among other canards. Despite the focus of the clinics bearing her name today, she was anti-abortion, and identified herself as a eugenicist, falling out with her own son when he fecklessly married a woman with poor eyesight. She was incontrovertibly extreme and many of her views are completely unacceptable by today's standards, but her primary cause ultimately improved the lot of millions of women. She died of breast cancer in 1958, but the charity Marie Stopes International developed in the 1970s to carry on her pioneering work, and it remains the leading family planning clinic in the UK, with outposts across the world too.

We can all thank Marie, and the scientific pioneers who developed effective contraception,* that we don't have to look forward to a life of relentless childbirth and clap. Given the options available today, if you are out there getting jiggy, there really is no excuse not to look after your uterus: whether it be via pill, condom, implant, coil, those weird femidom things or the

---

* Shout out to you, Margaret Sanger, Gregory Pincus, Carl Djerassi, Katherine McCormick, Richard Richter and all you other helpful chemists, biologists and campaigners.

delightfully seventies retro diaphragm. Choose your weapon. And if you find yourself in 'a bit of trouble', don't panic – thanks to the tireless campaigning of one woman who was prepared to speak up for her own bits and others', most of us do have a choice in the twenty-first century; and it's a tragedy that some of our very near neighbours still don't. However you decide to conduct your reproductive self-care, remember it's your body, and you should never let a dick in either the bedroom or the seat of power tell you what to do with it. Remember: sex is beautiful, reproduction is optional.

Betty Ford
and
Knowing When to Stop

(1918–2011)

'Too much of a good thing can be wonderful,' said the indomitable Mae West, but how do you know when your good boozy times are leading to bad? When can you tell you're having too many mornings-after-the-night-before? In general, we are getting wasted less than previous generations, but – downer alert – alcohol misuse is still the biggest risk factor for death and disability for fifteen- to forty-nine-year-olds in the UK. Beyond the perennial chart-topper booze, one in five sixteen- to twenty-four-year-olds still does a fair bit of smoking, snorting and munching on narcotics, predominantly the three graces of cannabis, cocaine and ecstasy (or Sleepy, Chatty and Horny, as Snow White would call them).

First Lady Betty Ford, one of the nicest Republicans you could meet, would come to understand the line between healthy and unhealthy assisted relaxation better than anyone. Elizabeth Anne Bloomer was born in Chicago. Her father was a salesman who died when she was sixteen, and her mother became an estate agent to keep the family afloat. Betty had a talent for dancing (see Mekatilili wa Menza on p. 95), starting lessons when she was eight and going on to work in Martha Graham's famous company in New York. Her mother wasn't 100 per cent sold on this career choice for Bets though, and she sounds like a formidable figure. When Betty was a plump little girl her mother stuck a sign to her daughter's back saying, 'Please do not feed this child'. Betty returned home to Grand Rapids, Michigan, where she worked as a model and fashion buyer, and ran a dancing school for marginalised children. In 1942 she married, but this union only lasted for five years. Not long after her divorce she met local lawyer Gerald Ford.

Gerald was on the campaign trail seeking office while the couple courted – and was in fact late for their wedding because of work. After he was elected, they moved to Washington. Betty stayed at home coping with the stresses of looking after their four children while Gerald was busy politicking. Betty began, like many mothers of young kids, to look forward to her unwinding tipple: which usually came at 5 p.m., although she also later recalled occasionally slipping tablespoons of vodka into her cups of tea during the day. In 1960 she suffered from a trapped nerve which led to a reliance on pain medication too. Betty started therapy, and her husband promised to resign his vice-presidency at the end of President Nixon's next term.

The family's plans to ease up were derailed by the Watergate scandal, which led to Nixon's resignation in 1974 and Gerald stepping up to be President in his place. That same year Betty had a mastectomy to treat breast cancer and took the very unusual step of going public. She encouraged hundreds of other women to have check-ups and instigated an unprecedentedly candid approach to her role as First Lady. Things were still pretty buttoned up in seventies America and people were scandalised by her admission that she and Gerry shared a bedroom in the White House, let alone by her support of abortion and gun control, her discussion of how open she'd be to her daughter having premarital sex or smoking weed, and, later, her frank conversations about her face-lift and her support of same-sex marriage. Conservative commentators dubbed her 'No Lady' rather than First Lady (see Phoolan Devi on p. 113) but many were also charmed by her openness and the way she cut the rug at state parties, and in 1975 she was voted *Time* magazine Woman of the Year. She became so popular that when her husband ran for a new term in 1975, supporters wore 'Vote for Betty's husband' badges. When Ger lost to Jimmy Carter the family retired to California.

All the while, Betty's dependence on drink and sleeping pills crept quietly on, intensifying finally to the point that in 1978 her daughter staged a family intervention and she went into rehab, much against her will. Even today, prominent people are inclined to keep breakdowns of this nature private, but Betty wasn't feeling that. She spoke publicly about her addictions, talking about how the pressure of raising her family and her feelings of inadequacy about not having a degree (see Isabella Beeton on p. 147) had sent her off the rails. She also put her money where her mouth was and in 1982 opened the first Betty Ford Center to treat addictions, aiming to help attendees become 'clean and serene'. Illustrious alumni include Liz Taylor, Ali MacGraw, Johnny Cash and Tony Curtis. She continued to travel and speak about addiction but stopped making public appearances after her husband's death in 2006. Betty died in 2011, aged ninety-three, and is buried next to him in the Gerald Ford Museum grounds in Grand Rapids.

Try to be as honest with yourself as Betty was with everyone else, when it comes to thinking about whether you're partying too hard. Having non-alcoholic days gives you an idea of how much you're relying on external props to have a good time. It's natural to occasionally long for a stiff drink after a hard day but if you're at risk of hurting yourself or other people when under the influence then it's fair to say that things have definitely gone too far. Make sure you have good friends who'll be frank with you, and listen to what they say. Happily, thanks in part to

Betty's work, getting help is no longer stigmatised the way it used to be and there are plenty of options to choose from. So raise a glass of mineral water to Betty, and keep on dancing!

Isabella Beeton
and
Beating Impostor Syndrome

(1836–1865)

Ah, Impostor Syndrome – pernicious underminer of talented people everywhere. No matter how brilliant your marks are, no matter what professional coups you pull off, deep down inside you believe all compliments are lies, and that you are only one mistake from being 'found out'. Infuriatingly, it's the talentless meatheads lacking an iota of charisma who are virtually guaranteed never to feel a tickle of this dreaded paranoia. In fact, it is usually high-achievers who are afflicted with this treacherous condition. So how to deal with it? There's one historical homemaker who perhaps *ought* to have felt Impostor Syndrome rather more keenly than most, but seems to have laughed in the face of her own ineptitude and achieved more in her short life than most of us can hope to over many years.

Think of Mrs Beeton and immediately an image comes to mind of a matronly lady in crinoline skirts, pudding bowl in hand, shouting at the servants and issuing draconian domestic decrees. And it's true that in her famous *Book of Household Management* Mrs Beeton was fond of such guff as: 'I have always thought that there is no more fruitful source of family discontent than a housewife's badly-cooked dinners and untidy ways', and 'When a mistress is an early riser, it is almost certain that her house will be orderly and well managed. On the contrary, if she remain in bed till a late hour, then the servants, who, as we have observed, invariably acquire some of their mistress's characteristics, are likely to become sluggards.' Lay off, Mrs B. Some of us need our lie-ins.

In fact, Isabella Beeton was a young, forward-thinking entrepreneur, translator, journalist and editor who – wait for it – was rubbish at cooking. Born in London, Izz was the eldest of twenty-one children. In 1856 she married the publisher Samuel Beeton and began to write articles for his monthly rag, the *Englishwoman's Domestic Magazine*. Her first contributions were columns on 'Cookery, Pickling and Preserving', which proved a massive hit, even though she forgot to add flour to the recipe for her 'Good Sponge Cake' and had to print an apology the following month. In fact, Mrs Beeton nicked many of her recipes. Having been advised by her aunt that culinary expertise took years to develop, she cherry-picked the best recipes from the books around her, benefitting from the very lax copyright laws at the time. Mrs B. has been accused of plagiarism over the years but she did come up with one innovation – listing ingredients at the beginning of the recipe so the cook could have everything they needed in front of them from the off. (She didn't mention measuring everything neatly into aspirational ceramics and Kilner jars, like on *Bake Off*, but we're sure she would have approved.)

Realising he had hot property on his hands, Isabella's husband Sam, ever the opportunistic publisher, decided to release a companion publication, and *Mrs Beeton's Book of Household Management* was born. It was a runaway bestseller and is still in print today, more than 150 years after publication. Its success lay in the fact that it was not just a book of two thousand recipes – it was also full of essays on domestic issues from menu-planning, to dealing with servants and child-rearing, and that evergreen essential, the 'Natural History of Fishes'. More practically, there is even a chapter from a doctor on illnesses, and from a lawyer advising on land boundary disputes and the like. Although Isabella has come in for much criticism over the years, her book is admirably aimed at teaching families to be frugal, and about seasonality and thrift. Growing industrialisation meant that, for the first time, many women did not live near their relatives, and while they could play a pretty tune on the piano, they hadn't a clue when it came to the complex demands of domestic organisation. Isabella compared running a household to commanding an army. (Perhaps we should substitute the cosy terms 'Housewife' and 'Homemaker' with 'Domestic Administrator' and

'Director of Home Affairs'.) Mrs B. showed the muddled mistresses of her generation what to do.

Isabella died at the shockingly early age of twenty-eight, after contracting an infection during the birth of her fourth child. After her death her fame grew; her book was constantly updated and given as a wedding present, and it remains a fixture on people's groaning cookery shelves even today. What's extraordinary is that this dynamic, unconventional twenty-something with very few culinary skills grew into a brand name that is still a byword for homemaking perfection. So if you are suffering from Impostor Syndrome look to this lady, the original domestic goddess, even though she was anything but. She *was* an impostor, and she still styled it out; she understood that the path to success lies in taking risks, accepting your limitations and realising that your flaws are no barrier to being completely amazing. And next time you're struggling at 7.45 a.m. trying to find some unladdered tights and your only other waterproof shoe, while downing your scalding cup of tea and answering emails on your phone, remember her key piece of lifehack advice: 'a place for everything, and everything in its place'.

George Eliot
and
Not Being Hot

(1819–1880)

The novelist Henry James was twenty-six when he first met the genius George Eliot, and she was fifty: 'She is magnificently ugly – deliciously hideous. She has a low forehead, a dull gray eye, a vast pendulous nose, a huge mouth, full of uneven teeth and a chin and jawbone *qui n'en finissent pas.*' Steady on HJ, it's not like you were a stud either. Because of this famous description, and the portraits we have of this most pre-eminent of novelists, reference to her looks has often accompanied appraisal of her literary works.

Mary Ann Evans was born in Warwickshire. Her father recognised the exceptional abilities of his clever and serious daughter, and made sure she had a good education – until her mother died when she was sixteen and she had to return home to look after the house. This was a typical retrograde step for young women of this era: it was expected that unmarried daughters would devote themselves to their dads. What was the point of you, after all, if you weren't looking after a man? But the stars aligned to feed little Mary Ann's discerning soul: her father's job managing the Arbury Hall Estate, and the kindness of the lady of the manor, gave her access to the extensive Hall library. Ever resourceful, she continued her studies on her own.

Once her sister and brother had both married their way out of the nest, Mary Ann was her father's sole companion. The Evanses were a religious family, concerned with social issues like assisting the poor of their parish, so Mary Ann was not much bothered with vanity, although she was aware that she wasn't a stunner. Intellectually, however, she was a gorgeous blossoming flower. When she and her father moved to Coventry, she found hip new friends in the Bray family, who introduced her to newfangled radical ideas, much to her dad's discomfort. She also embarked on a career in journalism, writing articles for the local paper owned by Mr Bray.

In 1849, when she was thirty, Mary Ann's father died, and she wasted no time in heading for the bright lights of the big city. Five days after the funeral she struck out for Europe and, on her return, moved to London, to lodge with the publisher John Chapman. He gave her a job as Assistant Editor of his periodical, the *Westminster Review*, a powerful position which she enjoyed for several years. Chapman's wife and mistress (predictably enough the kids' nanny) took against Mary Ann and John's interest in her and she was literally sent to Coventry for a while. However, it was not Chapman who would become Mary Ann's great love.

In 1851 she met the writer George Henry Lewes and they fell truly, madly, deeply in love. The one fly in the ointment was that George was, through a quirk of law, irrevocably married to someone else. His wife Agnes was living with a pal of his, and had several children by said chum, which George had officially agreed to declare were his. This amounted to condoning her adultery and made divorce impossible. So pious goody-two-shoes Mary Ann enraged her brother and started living in sin with her beloved. The following years of not being invited to dinner for being a slag proved immensely profitable for Mary Ann's career.

In 1857, aged thirty-seven, and encouraged by George, she published her first fiction, the story 'The Sad Fortunes of the Reverend Amos Barton', under the pen name George Eliot. It was a tremendous success. She chose a man's pen name to make sure the piece was taken seriously, and to avoid the scrutiny of marital status and physical attractiveness that female writers are still subject to. 'Amos' became the first part of her book, *Scenes of Clerical Life* (1858). This was followed by *Adam Bede* (1859), *The Mill on the Floss* (1860), *Silas Marner* (1861), *Romola* (1862), *Felix Holt* (1866), *Middlemarch* (1871) and *Daniel Deronda* (1876) – a remarkable hit rate by anyone's reckoning. *Middlemarch* is a magnificent book which regularly tops lists of Britain's greatest novels, and readers today are just as wowed by George's psychological insight as they were when it was first published. Her fans included Charles Dickens, Emily Dickinson (see p. 107) and Queen V. herself (see p. 289). After *Adam Bede*, George Eliot's true identity was eventually revealed but her scandalous living arrangements did nothing to dim her popularity. On the J. K. Rowling-like proceeds from George (E.)'s writing the couple bought a house near Regent's Park, where they lived very contentedly until George (L.)'s death in 1878.

Utterly bereft, the grieving writer devoted herself to her husband's memory. However, over the next few years she became increasingly close to a pal of her and George called John Cross. Kicking convention to the kerb once again, Mary Ann married him in 1880, despite the fact that he was twenty years younger than her. Their honeymoon in Venice was somewhat traumatic as John jumped out of a window into a canal but a happier result was her rapprochement with her brother now that she had finally, at the age of sixty, become a respectable married lady. Their reunion did not last long, as later that same year Mary Ann died of kidney failure. She is buried next to her dear George in Highgate Cemetery.

George Eliot was not a looker. So what? She had a fantastic career, a lifelong love and a bit of spicy cougar action just before her death, proving you don't need to be young or hot to get laid. And as Henry

157

James continued in his letter dissing her face: 'Now in this vast ugliness resides a most powerful beauty which, in a very few minutes steals forth and charms the mind, so that you end as I ended, in falling in love with her . . . Yes behold me literally in love with this great horse-faced bluestocking.' A disrespectful way to refer to a literary legend, to be sure, but this bluestocking lived a life full of passion and achievement: what a wonderful horse-faced model for all womankind she was.

Odette Sansom
and
Styling It Out

(1912–1995)

W e've all been there. That terrible sinking feeling when you've just hit 'reply all' and realise that you've mistakenly broadcast your bellyaching about a crap colleague to the whole office; or when instead of telling your workmate that you've decided a candidate will not be getting the job because you can't bear their shoes, you've told the sartorially challenged applicant themselves. In the twenty-first century, 'send' can be the first of a string of four-letter words. But for Odette Sansom, supplying information to the wrong recipient turned out to be a boo-boo with life-changing repercussions.

Odette Marie Céline Brailly was born in northern France. Her father was a decorated war hero killed in action in World War I; Sansom recalled in an interview that every Sunday she visited his grave with her young brother, and her grandfather reminded them that, should war come again, it would be their duty to emulate their father. Today's child psychologists would baulk at this heavy burden of responsibility, but even then Odette was made of stern stuff. As a child she overcame many illnesses including one that left her virtually blind for two years. In 1931 she married Roy Sansom, an English hotelier, moving to London with him after the birth of their first child.

At the outbreak of World War II, Roy enlisted, and, after the night bombings of the Battle of Britain turned London into a war zone, Odette moved to an idyllic village in Somerset with her mother-in-law and three daughters. It was there that she heard a BBC radio broadcast from the Admiralty asking for holiday photographs of France's northern coastline. The Luft-waffe controlled French airspace, so the RAF need-ed the snaps to help plan their bombing raids. Odette posted her pictures along with a note explaining that she was French and knew the area like the back of her hand. She sent the precious envelope to the Navy by accident, who then forwarded it to the Army, where it found its way to the Special Operations Executive (SOE). They immediately identified her potential as an agent. But would she be prepared to risk her life, given her young children? How would she cope if cap-tured and tortured?

Initially she was horrified by the idea and the thought of leaving her children. But reports of the suf-fering of those in occupied France persuaded her to agree to the training. She was taught all the fun stuff: Morse code, how to handle firearms, self-defence and resisting interrogation. Her final report was glowing, though it did list her main weakness as 'a complete unwillingness to admit that she could ever be wrong'

161

– a trait we applaud, particularly when dealing with the fallout of a bungled email. (In our defence, shoes maketh the woman.)

Agent S.23, code name Lise, arrived in Cannes in 1942 and was put to work in the Resistance by Peter Churchill, code name Raoul. Less than six months later, they were betrayed by someone inside the group. On their capture, they concocted a story that they hoped might protect them: that they were married (in fact, they were by this point lovers) and that Peter was the nephew of the famous Winston. Odette took full responsibility for any wrongdoing, insisting that her 'husband' was oblivious to her undercover activities. She was subjected to terrible torture – her toenails were torn out and her back was burned with hot irons.

Eventually her captors realised she wasn't going to squeal, so they sentenced her to death and she was transported to Ravensbrück concentration camp in 1944. The camp commandant believed her ruse about the Churchill connection and thought he had hostage gold on his hands. Odette was held in solitary confinement but, as the Allied forces closed in, the commandant escaped, taking her with him in his car, hoping to use her to bargain with the Americans. When she was finally handed over in May

1945, Odette immediately told her liberators who the commandant was and what he'd been responsible for – and she even managed to grab incriminating documents from his car. She later testified against him.

Amazingly, Peter Churchill also survived the war, and when he and Odette returned to London, Odette divorced Roy and married him (only to divorce him later and marry another SOE agent). Plucky Ms Sansom was awarded an MBE and was the very first woman to be awarded the George Cross for gallantry. A film was made of her life, and she and Peter visited the set – it's said the interrogation scenes were so vivid that this was the only time she broke down and wept. She died in 1995 at the ripe old age of eighty-two, an icon of bravery, resistance and all-round warrior womanhood. A housewife turned hard-as-nails agent. And all because of an epistolary error.

Sophia Duleep Singh
and
Embracing Your Discomfort Zone

(1876–1948)

There's no getting away from the fact that our world is one of astonishing levels of economic inequality: the globe's wealthiest 1 per cent own half of the world's riches. Just take a second to read that statistic again. Even if you're a few ponies short of a billion, it's important to realise how fortunate we are to live in a rich nation with a welfare state, and to try to figure out how we can make a positive difference to the world. There's a long line of women through history for whom resting on their gold-plated laurels was simply never an option. Take Sophia Duleep Singh – the suffragette you have never heard of – who, rather than settling for the usual life of a dog-breeding debutante, decided to grasp her destiny and challenge the injustices she saw all around her.

Born a royal, transformed into a revolutionary, Sophia was a woman of glorious contradictions. She had a wildly privileged upbringing: as the daughter of the Maharaja of Punjab, Princess Sophia grew up on the estate of Elveden in Suffolk, where cheetahs and leopards prowled the menagerie and peacocks strutted the lawn. She was introduced at court when she came of age and, on the death of her father (alone, in Paris and entirely broke), Sophia and her sister Bamba were given a 'grace and favour' apartment at Faraday House on Hampton Court Green, by her godmother, who just happened to be Queen Victoria (see p. 289). There she enjoyed all the trappings of aristocracy: feeding her dogs a diet of brandy and steak, and becoming a famous bike-riding fashionista – she was especially fond of her Columbia Model 41 Ladies' Safety Bicycle.

So far, so society. But then a trip to India in 1903 stirred Sophia's conscience; she was appalled by the dreadful poverty and inequality she witnessed there. She returned home looking for a cause to fight for, and she found it in the Women's Social and Political Union, the women-only campaign group led by Emmeline and Christabel Pankhurst (see p. 79) that pressed for women's right to vote in Edwardian England. These ladies were media-savvy – they knew how to catch a headline.

Princess Sophia went out of her way to be an embarrassment to the establishment. She was a proud member of the Women's Tax Resistance League, which refused to pay tax on the basis that, without the vote, a woman had no control over where those taxes would be spent. She sold copies of *The Suffragette* outside Hampton Court Palace, and she even threw herself at the Prime Minister's car, but despite all these attempts she couldn't get herself arrested. Those in power worked hard to keep her activities under wraps

– they were deeply squeamish about chucking the Queen's god-daughter into the slammer. 'Can anything be done to stop her?' asked one sitting MP, to which our response is a resounding 'Hell, no.' She spent her life funding the efforts of those fighting for women's suffrage, and we are proud to walk in her footsteps. Sophia is a shining example of a woman on a mission, despite the stifling trappings of her high social class and status. Grasp a cause, as Sophia did, and then agitate, agitate, agitate. Don't be afraid to leap from the snuggly cushions of your carefully *hygge*d comfort zone: a little bit of discomfort is often necessary on the way to the achievements you'll end up most proud of in your life.

Althea Gibson
and
Finding Your Mentor

(1927–2003)

Christian Dior and Yves Saint Laurent. Maya Angelou and Oprah Winfrey. Mr Miyagi and The Karate Kid. The greatest partnerships are often between mentor and mentee. Nowadays most employers have some kind of mentoring scheme, but if you feel like rolling your eyes at what looks like another of your HR department's meaningless buzzwords *du jour*, reconsider: it's true that inspiring and extraordinary people have usually been inspired by someone extraordinary in turn. Mentors can take many forms: teachers, parents, friends, colleagues or even lovers (see Akiko Yosano on p. 37), but what all of them offer is motivation and the knowledge that someone, somewhere has got your back. Oh, and they are also there to talk us round when we're about to make a great big cock-up.

Althea Gibson, Amazonian tennis warrior and the first black woman to smash it at Wimbledon, had a remarkable string of mentors who materialised at pivotal moments to cheer her on. Althea was the oldest of five children and endured a tough upbringing in Harlem in the 1930s. Her family was cash-challenged, and Althea found school hard-going, often playing hooky to ride the subway instead. Sport offered her an escape. She happened to live on a street designated a Police Athletic League area, which meant that during the day it was closed off so that kids could play sports (we applaud this idea for getting kids on to the streets, not off them).

Althea was built for tennis: five feet eleven inches in her flats and long-limbed, she had the reach and power great hitters need. After she became New York City Paddle Women's Champion at the age of twelve, her neighbours raised the money for her to compete at the American Tennis Association (ATA), where she won the junior national championship when she was seventeen. The ATA was the alternative to the United States Lawn Tennis Association (USL-TA), which at the time banned black players. It was here that she was spotted by Dr Walter 'Whirlwind' Johnson, or Dr J. to his protegees (who would later include fellow Wimbledon champion Arthur Ashe). Dr J. made sure Althea intensified her training and coached her personally himself. Billy Davis, the ATA men's champion at the time, recommended she train with Sydney Llewellyn, a bruising but stimulating fellow whom she married many years after their eyes first met over the net. But she was still barred from competing in the USLTA. Then Alice Marble, a white quadruple US champion, took up Althea's cause in a shaming letter to *American Lawn Tennis* magazine, asking why, if she was that damned good, wouldn't her fellow white sportswomen do her the honour of competing against her? 'It so happens,' Alice wrote, 'that I tan very easily in the summer – but I doubt that anyone ever questioned my right to play in the Nationals because of it.'

In 1950 Althea was finally invited to compete in what is now the US Open; although she was eliminated in the quarterfinals, her time was coming. Six years later she aced the singles title at the French Open, making history by becoming the first African-American player – male or female – to win a Grand Slam tournament. The following year she took Wimbledon and then – at last! – the US Open, repeating that double whammy in 1958. Advantage, Gibson!

In 1958, at the top of her game, Althea retired. She had peaked, and on a more prosaic level she was skint – there was no prize money back in those days, and no sponsorship either. Plus, she had so much more to give the world. In the following years she had a go at being a singer, acted in a Western (alongside John Wayne), joined the Harlem Globetrotters, playing exhibition matches before their games, and wrote two autobiographies, *I Always Wanted to Be Somebody* and *So Much to Live For*. She also became the first black member of the Ladies Professional Golf Association – breaking through in yet another exclusively white elite sport. She even ran in the 1977 Democratic

172

primary for a seat in the New Jersey Senate, coming second, and she enjoyed a long career directing and managing recreation programs in New Jersey.

But Althea always struggled with money and, in later life, health issues, falling victim to America's brutal health care system. This time her former doubles partner, Angela Buxton, stepped into the fray to help her out. British Buxton had herself overcome massive prejudice when, as a young Jewish woman, she was rejected by one of London's best clubs. She battled on and by 1955 was ranked number nine in the world. But could she find a doubles partner? Could she hell. So at the 1956 French Open these two outsiders found themselves thrown together – the ensuing partnership would prove totally boss: they scored a win in the doubles final in France, and a few weeks later took the Wimbledon doubles title. In 2001 the increasingly reclusive Althea called Angela to tell her how ill she was and how isolated – she was considering suicide. Buxton went on a furious money-raising operation, which apparently resulted in over a million dollars to help her friend. Althea died in 2003 at the age of seventy-six. She had been elected to the International Tennis Hall of Fame in 1971, and also appeared on a commemorative stamp from the US Postal Service.

Althea had a ground-breaking career and while she knew she had the grit to go all the way, she was also thankful to those who backed her. 'I always wanted to be somebody,' she wrote. 'If I made it, it's half because I was game enough to take a lot of punishment along the way, and half because there were a lot of people who cared enough to help me.' In time she herself became a magnificent mentor – the great Venus Williams said she was honoured to have followed in her footsteps. So don't be shy; find that inspiring role model to help you win every drop-shot and lob life serves at you. Mentoring can take any form you like. Just ask your HR advisor for a formal hook-up with a colleague you think has it sussed, or collar a trusted work friend to bounce ideas off and seek their two-pennies' worth. And remember to return the favour to more junior people in your team or peers who might come to you for guidance. You may just be a Yoda in the making.

Elizabeth I
and
Punchy Public Speaking

(1533–1603)

Dry mouth? Check. Sweating palms? Check. Irrational fear you might throw up? Check. Voice all weird, squeaky and high? Check. Welcome to the ordeal of public speaking. Very few of us approach it with anything but a rising sense of dread. But if you can find a way to fight the fear the rewards that lie in store for you are rich indeed. We can look towards our own Good Queen Bess as an example of a woman who, operating in a world almost entirely dominated by men, used her oratorical swagger to cement her reputation and win people over.

Little Lizzy had a tricky start in life – she was two and a half when her dad, King Henry VIII, accused her mum, Anne Boleyn, of sleeping around and had her beheaded. Henry banished his toddler daughter from court and declared her a bastard (nice dad-skills) but Elizabeth still went on to become Queen in 1558 at the age of twenty-five, after the death of her sister Mary.

She inherited a country torn apart by religious conflict, and the first job on her queenly to-do list was to reinstate Protestantism. Using her persuasive interpersonal skills, her intelligence and her carefully stage-managed aura of authority, within a year she had radically changed the religious landscape. She sacked the Pope from his position as boss of English

Christianity, re-established the Church of England (with herself as its chief, natch), and asserted the view that it was not up to her to compel her subjects to religious conformity in the same way her sister had done (with much torture and burning along the way; Liz was clearly hoping to achieve a better epithet than 'Bloody'). Showing early signs of rhetorical flourish, she explained that she 'would not open windows into men's souls'.

Elizabeth was wildly clever, fluent in French, Greek, Latin and Italian, and enjoyed translating the classics and composing her own sonnets for larks. However, even for a massive overachiever like her it must have been intimidating to express her opinion in a room full of older, experienced, politically machinating men. She may have learned something of how to put on an imperial show from one of her top hobbies: Gloriana (as she was called by the poet Spenser) was a keen patron of the arts, and during her reign there was a unique flowering of English literature, particularly in drama – as well as Spenser and Shakespeare, other literary giants such as Marlowe and Kyd found their voices. Watching actors perform and learning from others' oratory are both terrific tips for improving your own skills.

The Virgin Queen's job meant that her private life was a matter of public interest. She had many suitors, and nixed countless offers of marriage. Her singleton status made Parliament jumpy about the question of the succession, and at one point they refused to grant her any more cash until she had betrothed herself to someone. She used her rhetorical moxie to show how peeved she was: 'At present it is not convenient; nor never shall be without some peril unto you and certain danger unto me.'

As well as holding her suitors at bay, Elizabeth also rebuffed numerous threats from abroad, most majestically with her triumphant victory against the Spanish Armada in 1588. Hostile relations between Protestant England and Catholic Spain reached a nadir with King Philip's attempt at invasion. Bess's appearance amongst her troops on the eve of battle at Tilbury bore all the hallmarks of her genius for swashbuckling and grandstanding. According to reports of the day she appeared on a grey horse (perfect for making her red hair pop), dressed in armour in the manner of firebrand rebel Queen Boudicca (see p. 7). Placing herself *with* her people, she became, in this instance, the ultimate motivational speaker. Famously she said: 'I know I have the body but of a weak and feeble woman; but I have the heart and stomach of a king, and of a king of England too.' This is the fiercest humblebrag we've ever heard – in one sentence she acknowledges what her soldiers may have been thinking and in the next entirely subverts it by placing herself, and her steely intentions and courage, right at the forefront of their minds as their leader.

Elizabeth clearly knew when to issue a beautifully aimed clapback, as well as when to wield a bit of sweet talk. Her final farewell to Parliament, known as the Golden Speech, a triumph of combining command with emotion, had them all in tears, most likely at this line: 'though you have had, and may have, many princes more mighty and wise sitting in this seat, yet you never had nor shall have, any that will be more careful and loving'. So the next time you are forced to deliver that tricky presentation to your CEO, remember the tough crowd Bess faced, and how she won enough people over for her reign to be called 'the Golden Age'. Perhaps your tenure in the Accounts department can be similarly remembered? And finally some tips. Apparently imagining your audience naked doesn't work, and is even a bit distracting. Alcohol, in small doses, will do no harm. Always bear in mind that worse things happen at sea (particularly if you are the Spanish Armada). Remember, 99 per cent of the time everyone watching is willing you on to smash it (or thinking about what they want for their dinner that evening). And finally: the more you do it the easier it becomes. So take a deep breath, puff your ruff up, and begin . . .

Agatha Christie
and
Getting Over Heartbreak

(1890–1976)

Literary powerhouse Dame Agatha Christie is the bestselling fiction writer *of all time*. Her crime novels, including those featuring her busybody detectives Hercule Poirot and Miss Marple, are famous the world over, and have been translated into more than one hundred languages. She is also the author of the hit play *The Mousetrap*, which has been running continuously in London's West End since 1952. Alongside this she wrote romance novels, won several awards and a DBE, and her books have been adapted for TV and film. However, success in work doesn't necessarily mean success in life. In fact, women who outshine their husbands often suffer for it. Agatha certainly did.

Agatha Mary Clarissa Miller was born in Torquay into an affluent household. As a child, she loved reading, as most blossoming authors do, and started writing stories in her teens. After her father died in 1901, Agatha and her mum became a tight-knit unit, living and travelling together. In 1912 she met the dashing pilot Archibald Christie, whom she married in 1914 but did not properly live with until after the end of World War I when he returned from service in France in 1918. During the war Agatha worked as a pharmacist in a hospital in Torquay. This experience, especially what she learned about poisons, would prove very useful in her later career. In her spare time she started writing her first detective novel, featuring the marvellously moustachioed Poirot, *The Mysterious Affair at Styles*. In 1919, she and Archie moved into their first flat in London and had their only child, Rosalind. The next year *Styles* was published and Agatha's life changed overnight.

Suddenly, dear Agatha was all the rage. She published a novel almost every year, and sometimes more, until 1976. The spondulicks rolled in and in 1925 the Christies bought a house in Berkshire which they called Styles after the book which paid for it. However, Archie was not terribly interested in his wife's métier, preferring to spend his time playing golf. The next year Agatha was poleaxed by the death of her beloved mother, and again Archie's response was to hit the links rather than dispense the hugs. In fact, he had begun an affair with a young secretary who liked golf more than Agatha, Nancy Neele, and one night in December he told Agatha he wanted a divorce.

What happened next, and why, has been the subject of conjecture ever since: a mystery that even Miss Marple would struggle with. Once Archie had swanned off to his girlfriend's house, Agatha kissed her daughter goodnight (leaving her in the care of the servants) and drove off. Her car was found the next day but Agatha was not. A huge media frenzy ensued, with speculation abounding that Archie had murdered his wife, or that she was trying to frame him for her murder *Gone Girl*-style, or that it was a publicity stunt to push sales of her most recent book.

Agatha's disappearance was front-page news internationally and hundreds of police officers were involved in the investigation. Arthur Conan Doyle even took one of her gloves to a psychic for help (thanks, Arthur). Eleven days later Agatha was discovered in what is now the Old Swan Hotel in Harrogate (which today holds an annual festival for fans of crime fiction in her honour). In a nod to her rival, she had checked in as Teresa Neele from South Africa and had had a lively old time, singing and playing the piano in the bar – quite unlike her usual shy, brownish, somewhat dowdy self. She didn't initially recognise Archie when he came to collect her and doctors diagnosed her with an amnesiac breakdown, which others have speculated was possibly caused by a concussion from crashing her car on the way to commit suicide. She recovered and she and Archie were finally divorced in 1928; he promptly married Nancy. Agatha treated herself to a trip on the Orient Express as her heartbreak holiday (see *Murder on the Orient Express* for the somewhat backhanded advertising she later gave this jaunt).

Agatha's star continued in its ascendancy, and she kept up her travels. On one excursion she met the archaeologist Max Mallowan, whom she married in 1930, moving on to a more settled life. During World War II she volunteered again in a hospital, and also wrote some of her best work. In 1956 she was awarded a CBE (and later made a dame) and the next year became President of the Detection Club, a society of crime writers where members pledged allegiance with this fabulous oath: 'Do you promise that your detectives shall well and truly detect the crimes presented to them, using those wits which it may please you to bestow on them, and not placing reliance on nor making use of Divine Revelation, Feminine Intuition, Mumbo-Jumbo, Jiggery-Pokery, Coincidence or Act of God.' In 1976 she died peacefully at home in Oxfordshire, leaving behind an unmatched literary legacy.

Agatha's books are often regarded as rather cosy, polite stories of murder, but are much more vicious and dark than this interpretation suggests. Her tweedy image is also undercut by the melodrama of her famous vanishing act on being ditched by her man. We can all learn a lesson from her behaviour in the aftermath. She made damn sure that her husband's infidelity was not going to go unnoticed, and he wasn't able to skip off to his bit-on-the-side for Netflix and chill without some severe public awkwardness. Although we don't endorse setting up your ex as a murderer, we do think that being dumped deserves a bit of drama and wallowing, and certainly a nice holiday to help you get over it. Who knows who you might meet on your travels? And, as a final aside about how Agatha was so much cooler than you might imagine, in the 1920s she became the first British woman to surf standing up, while travelling in South Africa. So golf can go fuck itself.

Grace Hopper
and
Facing Up to Failure

(1906–1992)

Computer pioneer and high-ranking Navy lady 'Amazing' Grace Hopper was so unbelievably impressive it feels a bit wrong to even breathe the word failure anywhere near her, but in fact she faced banana skins, frustration and her own shortcomings at many points over the course of her life. Born in New York, Grace was the oldest of three children, and like many of the wonderwomen in this book, she had a progressive papa who wanted to give his girls the same education as his boy. And her mum loved maths, which doesn't hurt when you're raising a science whizz. Always happiest when faced with a puzzle, it's said that at the age of seven Grace took an alarm clock to pieces to see how it worked. When she failed to put it together again she dismantled six other clocks to try to crack the enigma. Where the rest of us might have hidden the pieces and pointed the finger of blame at our little brother, onwards Grace went, undeterred.

After excelling at maths, physics, biology and chemistry at school, in 1923 Grace set her sixteen-year-old heart on attending the elite Vassar College, but failed her Latin exam and had to defer for a year. She knew her many talents didn't extend to languages, but realised perseverance would see her right, so she worked her arse off, successfully bagged herself a place a year later, and decided to study for a light and breezy double major in mathematics and physics. Grace wanted a job in engineering, but was savvy enough to realise that, at the time, few women stood a chance of succeeding in that sexy field, so she decided to become an academic, and after a Master's at Yale she returned to join the faculty at Vassar. She was a ridiculously good teacher and students flocked to her classes. A stellar mathlete, she also had a magpie mind which was drawn to different disciplines: she ended up auditing courses in physics, architecture, philosophy, economics, astronomy and geology, and became fluent in French and German, Latin and Greek. In your face, languages!

At this point the rest of us might have sat back, exhausted at the scale of our impressive Renaissance womanhood. But at 7.55 a.m. on 7 December 1941, 183 aircraft of the Imperial Japanese Navy attacked Pearl Harbor, killing 2,403 people. Grace was determined to join the war effort. But she was deemed underweight and overold – at thirty-four she was considered *ancient*: imagine! For some this would have been a nice excuse to give the military a miss, but Grace was not up for being a comfortable college professor in a time of conflict, and after much petitioning, she took herself off to the US Naval Reserve Midshipmen's School in Massachusetts.

Grace loved the rigidity of her military rigours and graduated first in class. Lieutenant Hopper was born. The Navy was desperate for mathematicians, – figuring out the trajectory of missiles gave them a massive advantage over the enemy – so they sent Grace to their Bureau of Ships Computation Project at Harvard University, where they were trying to build a machine that would be able to make speedy calculations about tricky variables like wind speed, distance and temperature. Here she came face to face with the Harvard Mark I Computer: a beast of a machine which was 15 metres long, 2.5 metres high, contained a staggering 530 miles of wires and couldn't even play *Angry Birds*. It worked on instruction from reams of perforated paper tape and there was no manual. She also met the research team leader Howard Aiken, a grumpy genius who is said to have welcomed her with the words 'Where the hell have you been?' Aiken ran his operation like the Navy outfit it was; everyone wore uniform and, crucially, rank was more important than gender. Grace set to work, staying late most nights, and managed to get the machine to do in minutes what would take the mind a year. She also produced a five-hundred-page manual for Mark along the way; a manual which became a blueprint for the principles of computer operations we use today.

Post-war, Grace stayed on as a research fellow on Aiken's team and pushed forward the field of programming. She was a key player in the efforts to replace mathematical symbols in coding with simple English terms – she claimed she only developed this since 'no one thought of that because they weren't as lazy as I was'. Meanwhile her naval career continued full speed ahead. In 1983 she was made Commodore by special presidential decree and two years later became one of the first female rear admirals. She retired on the deck of USS *Constitution* at the age of seventy-nine, died in 1992 and was buried with full military honours. In 1996 a naval destroyer was christened in her honour, the USS *Hopper*.

Grace Hopper was an exceptional brain working in a totally male-dominated world. She knew that failure is inevitable, and therefore nothing to be frightened of; and that it's how you deal with the adversity life chucks at you that is important. The act of facing up to our loserdom can sometimes hold the key to success – and in fact the endless pursuit of triumph can contribute to unhappiness. Resting on your laurels, rather than trying something new is much worse than failing, and as the lady herself famously said: 'The most dangerous phrase in the language is, "We've always done it this way."' Truly amazing, Grace.

Sheila Michaels
and
Calling Yourself Ms

(1939–2017)

Meet Mr John Smith. Tell me what you know about him. How old is he? How desperate is he? Is he married? Is he divorced? Is he a traditional kind of guy or more of an outlier? Is he a teacher? There's no way for you to guess. Sphinx-like Mr Jones doesn't have a single thing in his name that reveals details about his private life. But what about Mrs John Smith, or Mrs Emma Smith, or Miss Emma Smith or Ms Emma Smith? There are some conclusions our conscious and unconscious bias might lead us to draw from how she chooses to fill in her credit card forms. Do we really want people to be able speculate on this information, however lightly? The history of the honorifics applied to women is an interesting one that throws up lots of chewy food for thought.

Back in ye olden days it was relatively simple: most people didn't get an honorific at all, they were just John or Emma Smith. But there were the dukes and marchionesses to consider, and the insidious British love of a bit of class stratification. Middle-class men were called Master, which developed into Mister for adults (but stayed as Master for young men), then abbreviated to plain old Mr, which was straightforward, universal and done and dusted for all time. It's much trickier to get a handle on our sisters' sobriquets. But here goes: originally all adult women in polite society or the trades were called Mistress (either of their servants or their trade), abbreviated to Mrs (and later both Miss and Ms indiscriminately), up until the eighteenth century when Miss started to be used for younger women and Mrs for older, with marital status irrelevant. But by the end of the nineteenth century, Mrs started to mean married, and Miss unmarried (and in fact calling an adult Miss was a sly burn implying she was a prostitute). At this point of course if you were a Miss you were assumed to be the responsibility of your father and, if you were a Mrs, of your husband: hence the erasure involved in becoming Mrs John Smith, which is still considered perfectly reasonable in posh etiquette handbooks. At various points in the twentieth century being Mrs *Emma* Smith would imply you were divorced. So confusing, unnecessary and invasive!

Thank goodness there are sensible alternatives available. In France they've got rid of all the mimsy Mademoiselle stuff and gone for just one basic 'Madame' for everyone. In 1901 in the US they came up with Ms as a catch-all that avoided any focus on a woman's personal life: 'The abbreviation "Ms." is simple, it is easy to write, and the person concerned can translate it properly according to circumstances. For oral use it might be rendered as "Mizz," which would be a close parallel to the practice long universal in many bucolic regions, where a slurred Mis' does duty for Miss and Mrs. alike."* However, Ms didn't catch on until a New York radio broadcast in 1969 by feminist activist Sheila Michaels in which she talked about the term.

Sheila had personal reasons to be drawn to Ms, which she first discovered on the address label of a friend's Marxist magazine and initially assumed was a typo: 'I had never seen it before: It was kind of arcane knowledge.' Sheila was born in St Louis, the product of her mother and her boyfriend Mr London, but was raised by her mother's husband, Mr Michaels, until they divorced and her mother remarried Mr Kessler, who gave Sheila his surname, before withdrawing it years later when he disapproved of her activism and she reverted to Michaels. Are you keeping up? When she married her husband, Hiraku Shiki, she became Sheila Shiki-y-Michaels. (For discussion of keeping your maiden name see Amelia Earhart on p. 253.) You can see why she was drawn to a less complicated and loaded form of address. She later said she was 'looking for a title for a woman who did not "belong" to a man. There was no place for me.'

* *Springfield (Mass.) Sunday Republican* 10 November 1901, 4/5.

After Sheila brought Ms. to prominence over the airwaves during a discussion about feminism on liberal radio station WBAI, the new term influenced Gloria Steinem, who used it as the title for her iconic feminist magazine for modern women, which launched in 1972.

Sheila had a varied life: she was expelled from college for her civil rights activism, moved to New York in 1959 and went on to be a campaigner, writer, restaurateur and taxi driver. Her lasting legacy remains the raising of awareness about how women project their own identities and choices into the world. The simplest thing would obviously be for us to go back to the old zero-honorific days, but given that every online form everywhere requires you to pick from Mr, Mrs, Ms, Miss, Dr, Revd, HRH, His Holiness, etc., the next simplest is to just get a PhD or go for Ms. In fact, we'd go further and advocate for the more recent Mx, which was invented in the 1970s to cater for those who don't wish to state either their relationship status or their gender, and is accepted by the UK government in all its correspondence. Whatever you choose, and you can choose whatever you damned like, be aware of its historical significance and Ms Michaels's part in broadening your options and safeguarding your privacy. She freed us up to concentrate on the important stuff, like expressing our wit and essence in our Twitter handles instead.

Soraya Tarzi
and
Closing the Domestic Divide

(1899–1968)

Finding a person with whom you can share a balanced partnership should be right up there in your #relationshipgoals. For most of us today the division of responsibility, love and labour is assumed to be pretty equal (ignoring the boringly tenacious fact that in heterosexual couples women do almost 40 per cent more housework than men), though we know some of our sisters elsewhere in the world have a much rougher deal. It certainly wasn't always this way: in most societies before the twentieth century men oversaw the money, decisions and the fate of the world, and women oversaw the cleaning, kids and soft furnishings. In some places this is depressingly still the norm and men are cruelly deprived of embroidery opportunities even now. You might be surprised to find out that back in the 1920s Afghanistan was a hotbed for a bit of progressive ladydom.

Soraya Tarzi was born in Syria just as the nineteenth century ended, to a powerful Afghan family who had been exiled from their homeland. Her papa was a cosmopolitan intellectual titan, sometimes referred to as the father of Afghan journalism. The Tarzis came back into favour and the court in Kabul, when the new emir, Habībullāh Khan, took over. Young Soraya caught the eye of the emir's charming son, Amanullah, and the pair were married in 1913. Unusually

for their culture at this time, Amanullah was monog-
amous and didn't take any further wives.

Things were pretty tasty in Afghan politics at this
point and Habībullāh was assassinated in 1919, putting Amanullah in the hot seat at the age of twenty-
seven. He was a rapid moderniser – probably a bit
too rapid in hindsight – and Soraya supported him
in his reforming ambitions from the start. Cannily he
declared his country's independence from Britain in
his coronation speech, instantly endearing himself to
his people. He also told them: 'I am your king, but the
Minister of Education is my wife – your Queen.'

Soraya was a modern Muslim woman. She'd been
brought up in a liberal, open household, and that
wasn't going to change just because she was a queen.
She wore European-style clothes and was fond of
hunting on horseback. Early on in their reign, she did
wear a small, thin light-blue veil on her hat, but when
Amanullah gave a speech clarifying that Islam didn't
legislate on the matter of veils, she ditched it, with
the rest of the women present in the room at the time
apparently ripping theirs off to match her. She was a
vocal feminist and, thanks to her and her husband's
determination, in 1923 Afghan women were granted
equal rights with men. (It's worth noting that British
women only won equal voting rights with men five

years later.) Soraya was particularly fired up about education and she opened the first girls' school in her country, and a women's hospital as well. Famously she said: 'Independence belongs to all of us and that is why we celebrate it. Do you think, however, that our nation from the outset needs only men to serve it? Women should also take their part as women did in the early years of our nation and Islam.' By stressing that it was morally imperative that women learn and contribute on all levels, and linking this to Islam, she sought to head off the fury of the traditionalists, who were less than delighted with the way things were going.

Sadly, the infuriated mullahs really lost their shit when, after a trip to Europe, the royal duo began to talk about banning parents' control over their daughters' marriages. This, combined with photographs that were circulated (probably by the conniving British, who wanted to destabilise the region) of Soraya in sleeveless evening dresses with her hand being kissed by various foreign leaders, led to a simmering cauldron of reactionary ire. Aside from outrage about the affront to their cultural values, many dads were pissed off that they were going to lose out on bride prices (the opposite of dowries) if the marriage reforms went through. The ensuing revolt led to famed bandit leader

Bacheh Saqqāw staging a coup and taking Kabul. Amanullah abdicated in 1929 and the royals left for permanent exile in Europe.

OK, so Amanullah and Soraya didn't manage to replicate their equal partnership on a national scale, but they did achieve some extraordinary advances for women and girls in their short reign. And despite some backward steps, women's rights developed in fits and starts in Afghanistan on the back of their example, right up until the deeply disagreeable Taliban took charge in the 1990s. In 2004 the equal rights for men and women that Amanullah and Soraya had initiated decades earlier were finally reinstated.

Now, we aren't asking you and your boo to alter the culture and politics of an entire country, just to realise that seeing your partner as a teammate makes everything a hell of a lot more fulfilling. This isn't about being the same; in fact being able to agree to disagree on big things is a true sign of power parity. Don't worry if you can't reach a consensus on the rules of Scrabble or the setting on the thermostat. Things to watch out for are: do you bolster your beloved when they're down and get the same support when you need it? Do you both have a say in when, where and how sex happens? (Or, if not, have you at least both signed one of those *Fifty Shades* contracts?) Do you both make decisions about holidays, living expenses and what to watch on Prime? Do you take turns washing up? If any of these questions give you pause for thought, it might be time to consider whether the scales of your love need rebalancing. The best kind of affair is a fair affair.

Catherine the Great
and
Dealing with Gossip

(1729–1796)

It's far too easy to get saddled with a bad reputation these days – and for that rep to linger about on social media in perpetuity. Women seem to be magnets for judgement: we're either too fat or too thin; too frigid or too promiscuous; too weak or too strident. It takes a great deal of self-belief, flexibility and shaking it off to keep your chin up sometimes, without feeling like your past, or the haters, are dragging you down.

One lady who knew how to shape her personal brand was Catherine, Empress of All the Russias (not just the one, *all* of them). It's a testament to her tenacity that one of the most memorable Russian leaders of all time wasn't actually Russian, wasn't called Catherine and had no real right to the throne.

Sophie von Anhalt-Zerbst was born a Lutheran German princess in what is now Poland. Posh but poor, short but with a GSOH, she was shipped off to Russia by her family when she was fifteen to get engaged to her cousin, the ruling Empress Elizabeth's nephew and heir, Peter. Sophie converted to Russian Orthodoxy and changed her name to Catherine to signal her fresh start. The Russian court was rife with intrigue and political manoeuvring, and a savvy young Catherine kept her eyes and ears open, studying hard to learn the language – unlike Prussian* Pete who wasn't keen on his intended nation, or his intended bride. Returning the favour, Catherine referred to her fiancé as an 'idiot', so romance was never very much on the cards for these two. She and Peter married in 1745 but didn't have their first child, Paul, until nine years later. Rumours suggest that none of Catherine's four children was anything to do with Peter, and it is widely accepted that both parties had many affairs.

When Empress Elizabeth died in 1762, after twenty-one years in charge, Pete became Peter III: and thus began his less than illustrious six-month reign. Peter was very pro-Prussia, which was a dumb play at the time, given Russia was involved in the Seven Years' War against said nation. He immediately made peace, and instituted various reforms which aggravated many of his nobles. Catherine, who had made herself exceedingly popular at court, saw an opportunity and moved quickly to get the army on her side and arrest her husband. On 28 June 1762 she marched into St Petersburg with her soldiers and had herself proclaimed Empress, forcing Peter to abdicate in her favour. Not long after this, her

---

* Prussia was the kingdom that later developed into Germany – although its territory at different points also included parts of Poland, Russia and other modern-day countries.

boyfriend's brother murdered poor Pete. There is no hard evidence Catherine was involved in this act but it did cast a shadow over her reputation.

In 1773 Peter inconveniently, and miraculously, reappeared in the guise of the disgruntled Cossack Yemelyan Pugachev, who impersonated the dead Tsar in order to rouse a rebellion. Objecting to Catherine's rule, thousands of peasants rallied behind Pugachev, and her army only managed to stifle the revolt in 1775. It was a very fighty period, though there was love in the air too, as around this time Catherine found a new boyfriend in her advisor Grigory Potemkin. Their period working and sleeping together was very successful for Russia in its imperial expansion, although they didn't remain romantically exclusive for very long. Generally Catherine stayed friends with her many exes.

Even with rumours of her sexual profligacy swirling around, Empress C. went on to have an extremely successful career, by contemporary standards: she didn't get usurped or assassinated, and died a natural death. She was also known as 'the Great', which is pretty affirming, despite the fact that modern historians judge her to have been a harsh ruler who made life harder for her poorer subjects.

Catherine ruled for thirty-four years. She applied her boundless energy to expanding Russia's borders and colonising new territory, building up the state's coffers at the expense of the clergy, fiddling with and then nixing Poland, reforming local bureaucracy and state education (notably setting up the first educational establishment for girls: the Smolny Institute), pen-palling with international intellectuals like Voltaire, amassing an impressive art collection, and magnetically drawing all manner of scandal to herself, none of which stopped her from doing what she wanted.

The All-wise Mother of the Fatherland died of a stroke in 1796, and her death drew the most extravagant rumours of all: that she had copped it while shagging a stallion in a specially made stallion-shagging contraption. (It says a lot about the sexual standards of the day that just because she had a lot of boyfriends, people found it easy to believe that she would also be partial to a bit of bestiality.) This colourful piece of gossip puts in the shade the whispers that you got off with your best friend's bloke at a party, or that you have a funny-shaped boob, or that you fancy your physics teacher. Most importantly, Catherine wouldn't have given a flying horse-fuck about this rumour. She knew her energy, power and rather too modern approach to sleeping with whatever bright young men happened her way meant that people would talk. She's a splendid example of the potency of realising that not everyone is going to like you – and that's complete-ly OK. And also that your happiness doesn't rest in what other people think. 'I used to say to myself that happiness and misery depend on ourselves. If you feel unhappy, rise above it and act so that your happiness may be independent of all outside events.' Great, indeed.

Hedy Lamarr
and
Knowing Your Worth

(1914–2000)

Known in her day as the most beautiful woman in the world, screen siren Hedy Lamarr was also one of the smartest – though it took a while for the world to wake up to this genius wrapped in the guise of a goddess. It figures that the breathtakingly glamorous Hedy didn't use her birth name of Hedwig Eva Maria Kiesler when she took to the stage. Born in Austria into comfortable circumstances, Hedy was clearly a bright child and could speak several languages by the time she was ten years old, as well as being an accomplished pianist and dancer. She went to drama school in Berlin and from there managed to get stage work and bit parts in a few films before her big breakthrough came.

In a highbrow version of the Kardashian sex tape, nineteen-year-old Hedy's performance in the 1932 Czech film *Ecstasy* made her famous and infamous in one blow. Ahem. *Ecstasy* saw Hedy and her long-forgotten co-star in the first explicit sex scene in a widely released film, which went on to be banned in the US and denounced by the Pope. Her parents did not enjoy the premiere. There is nothing in the film that would widen modern eyes, but it does involve Ms Lamarr frolicking about starkers and acting out the sexual ecstasy of the title (the writhing in this scene was apparently achieved by the director poking Hedy's bum with a pin). It's a horrifyingly familiar industry tale: a teenage woman's body is her means of success, and is treated like property by the men she works with, but *Ecstasy* did launch Hedy on her celebrity career path. A path she later defined pithily: 'The ladder of success in Hollywood is usually a press agent, actor, director, producer, leading man; and you are a star if you sleep with each of them in that order.' (It's salutary to note that Hedy said this over fifty years ago and yet the movie business is only just starting to sort out its problem with predatory execs.)

However, Hedy's new-found starlight was almost immediately snuffed out by her possessive husband, the wealthy fascist arms manufacturer Fritz Mandl, who tried to round up all the prints of *Ecstasy* and destroy them. Hedy soon tired of his controlling ways and in 1937 wisely escaped: according to her account by disguising herself as a maid and sneaking out of their castle to flee to Paris and then London. Here she met Louis B. Mayer and signed a contract with MGM. Soon after, in 1938, she starred in her first English-language film, *Algiers*, and captivated audiences with her beauty. From this point on she was cast solely in exotic, seductive parts, which eventually frustrated her enough to leave MGM and set up her own company. However, 1949 saw her cast again as a glitzy ho with Cecil B. DeMille's smash hit *Samson and Delilah*, of which Groucho Marx charmingly said, 'I'm not interested in a film where the man's tits are bigger than the woman's,' encapsulating what we already know about a woman's role on the silver screen in the golden age of Hollywood.

However, our Hedy was certainly not just T and A – there was a singular brain residing in that beautiful head of hers, and World War II motivated her to new enterprises. With knowledge she gleaned from her time with her arms-dealing ex (who had failed to realise his wife was soaking up all manner of intel whenever the Third Reich top brass came to supper), she worked with the pianist George Antheil to come up with a frequency-hopping radio device to help missiles break through German blocking frequencies. Apparently her first conversation with George at a party started with them discussing the size of her boobs, but happily led on to more significant subjects.

Hedy and George gave their patent to the Navy for free but it wasn't exploited, until it later contributed to the technology that we now use every day in our mobile phones, Wi-Fi and GPS. Hedy loved inventing things, and during the war applied to the National Inventors Council but was rebuffed, and told that she could use her celebrity to raise money for the war effort instead.

She duly did this, once raising $7 million in one go, but she continued to indulge in creative pursuits in her spare time. Among the novelties she developed were new designs for traffic signals, tissue boxes, a fluorescent dog collar and a powdered fizzy drink cube.

It took until 1997, when Hedy was eighty-four, for her to be properly recognised as an inventor. She and George were given a Pioneer Award from the Electronic Frontier Foundation (on news of which she said, 'Well, it's about time'), and further honours followed, as well as a much broader awareness of the work Hedy did in her life that stretched beyond staring sultrily at a camera.

Only five years after finally becoming a US citizen in 1953, Hedy retired. She never quite left scandal behind her: she was divorced six times, arrested for shoplifting twice, sued the publishers of her own memoir and various others, and underwent extreme plastic surgery in her later years. She died aged eighty-six, still primarily lauded for her pulchritude rather than her scientific prowess. Smart-talking, smart-thinking, always curious and engaged in the world around her, the star Lamarr was so much more than just a pretty face. No one could rock a centre parting, a bold lipstick and an elegant understanding of spread-spectrum broadcast quite like Hedy. These days it's possible for people to conceive of a woman being capable of both beauty and brains. The important thing is to make the most of what you've got, be wise to society's prejudices, and, like Hedy, be clear on where you attribute your own value: 'Any girl can be glamorous; all you have to do is stand still and look stupid.'

Eleanor of Aquitaine
and
Managing Infidelity

(c. 1122–1204)

Infidelity is a tricky beast. It usually ends up with more than one person getting hurt, whichever side of the fuckaround you're on. In most cases, the damage is predominantly emotional, with a bit of added slutshaming if you're a woman. However, it remains an unforgiveable horror that in the twenty-first century people, particularly women, are still lawfully killed for adultery in some countries, a punishment actually *worse* than that faced by most women in the *Game of Thrones*-esque age of Eleanor of Aquitaine, over eight hundred years ago. (The typical medieval punishments were also nasty: having your nose cut off, your head shaved, being shamed through the streets, etc.)

For a woman of Eleanor's social and economic position, whether or not you had a bit on the side was a matter of great legal import, as well as of family reputation. Landowning husbands required a legitimate scion to pass their wealth on to, and an authentic heir required a wife who definitely kept her legs shut for anyone but the hubby. Without Jeremy Kyle kindly distributing paternity tests, the only way a man could rest easy that he wasn't bequeathing his ancestral wealth to the bastard son of the milkman was to believe wholeheartedly in his wife's unassailable virtue, or deny her any opportunity for mischief.

Eleanor of Aquitaine was not the sort of girl to be

denied anything. Fact and fiction about her are hard to disentangle, and as we know, feisty women in the olden days attracted accusations of immoral behaviour like flames to a heretic, so we can't be sure of the exact truth. Born in Poitiers in central France, she was a teenager when she inherited her father the Duke of Aquitaine's vast estate in 1137. King Louis VI, wisely immediately married her to his son, the imminent Louis VII who took the throne the same year. France's highly educated new Queen, fresh from the boho, arty Poitiers crowd where everyone was hanging out with the troubadours after their gigs, found frosty court life underwhelming. However, she loved the high-level political shenanigans. The couple had a daughter and then went on a romantic trip to Jerusalem in 1147, to lead the Second Crusade to liberate the Holy Land from Islamic control. As you do.

This was the undoing of the royal marriage. First off, Eleanor made a show of herself by leading her own troops, wearing armour. When they stopped off in Antioch to visit her Uncle Raymond, his chumminess pissed Louis right off. Rumours abounded that Eleanor and Ray were playing *se cacher la saucisse*. In 1149 they returned home from the worst family holiday ever: particularly given the Crusade failed and Raymond was killed in battle.

Eleanor styled out rumours of her adultery and the couple went on to have another child. However, Mr and Ms the Seventh were not happy new parents with another disappointing girl, and in 1152 their marriage was annulled on the grounds that they were too closely related. Louis kept their daughters and Aquitaine was given back to Eleanor. Two months later she cheekily married another relation, Henry of Anjou, whose father she was rumoured to have banged. She did this without Louis's permission, bringing all of western France under the English crown when her new groom became Henry II two years later. King L. must have been fuming when he heard this news.

Eleanor, in her early thirties, having polished up her political proficiency for fifteen years in France, brought all her experience to bear on queening England for the next fifty. She and Henry had a spirited relationship, resulting in eight children and many dust-ups. Their sons grew up hungry for power and their endless squabbling resulted in rebellion against Henry in 1173, which Eleanor supported. Henry pardoned his boys but kept Eleanor under house arrest for the next fifteen years.

Despite her own dodgy rep, Eleanor is said to have turned against Henry because of his profligate playing away. She is even rumoured to have murdered his favourite mistress, Rosamund, whom he was planning to marry (meaning divorce for our El). Gossip spread that Eleanor had tracked Rosamund down in the maze Henry had built for private nooky (classier than a Travelodge), and demanded that she choose death by poison or dagger.

However, Henry also annoyed Eleanor by meddling with Aquitaine affairs, so perhaps she just didn't like him touching her stuff. In any case, when Henry was succeeded consecutively by his sons Richard (of Lionheart fame) and John, Eleanor continued to exert her influence over the kingdom, running the joint when Richard was off crusading, and politicking her way across Europe in her late seventies to arrange advantageous marriages and defend Aquitaine from attack by her grandson (her family were exhaustingly dysfunctional). Finally, in 1202, she retired to Fontevraud Abbey, to rest on laurels that included being Duchess of Aquitaine, Queen of France, Queen of England, contender for most powerful woman in twelfth-century Europe, politician and patron of the arts. She died there in 1204.

So what can we learn from Eleanor about infidelity? Her alleged experience at both cheating and being cheated on shows that you need to have your endgame always in mind. Stepping out on Louis looks like a win: she got her property back and went on to what seemed like a better relationship, with more opportunities for her to live a full life exercising her talents. However, let's not forget those two daughters left back with her ex. There is always collateral damage. And if you're on the end of a sneaky bastard's two- or three-timing? Eleanor seems to have accepted Henry's shadiness until the risk of divorce came up, which would have changed her political position and that of her children: a proper existential threat. Faced with this, the dagger and the poison came out. We'd prefer to recommend some Relate therapy and cool-headed discussion of what you both stand to win or lose by moving on or moving forward. But obviously different rules apply if you're 'Eleanor, by the wrath of God, Queen of England', as she majestically referred to herself in a letter to the Pope.

Coco Chanel
and
Killing It at Work

(1883–1971)

Never discuss your children. But *do* talk about them when you are trying to bond with new clients. Adopt a friendly facial expression when having difficult conversations. But act like a man and be assertive too. Maintain direct eye contact, and a bit of a frown. Smile. Be confident and assertive, but also deploy your non-threatening feminine smarts. Make no mistake, there's a bewildering array of advice out there for the career gal trying to get ahead. From leaning-in to *savoir faire*-ing it seems women should be all things, all the time. It's enough to make you want to paint over that glass ceiling and head off slacker-backpacking around the world. Happily, Coco Chanel is on hand to show us another way.

Gabrielle Bonheur Chanel came forth into the world in less than glamourous style. She was born in a poorhouse in August 1883 (amazing to think this icon of cool was born in utter deprivation in the nineteenth century); her early history is murky, and, to make matters even murkier, Coco was as creative about her own backstory as she was with her designs. We do know she had two brothers and two sisters and that when her mother died of tuberculosis her father, in a sadly all too familiar show of bad-dad-dom, abandoned them. The girls were sent to a convent. When Coco turned eighteen she joined a religious order in Moulins in central France, where she was encouraged by the sisters to sew. The Mother Superior later secured Coco a job as a seamstress in town, where she had a great time gadding about with a group of soldier-boys, who took her out to music halls and cabaret bars. Free from the convent, Coco fancied life as a chanteuse – the song she became known for was 'Ko Ko Ri Ko', and so her nickname was born. Her singing career failed to launch, but by then she had fallen in with a playboy cavalry officer, Étienne Balsan, a saucy chap who kept racehorses. He would be her *billet* to the glamorous world of Paris. Through him she also met Boy Capel, an Englishman. This *ménage à trois* would develop into a sound business trio; Boy and Balsan were both her paramours, but they also provided the financial backing for Coco's first business selling hats in Paris in 1910.

From the start Coco was all about stripped-back style; she believed that over-adornment was very ageing, darling. Soon, business was booming, and Mme Chanel was extremely pleased with herself, but then Boy admitted that he hadn't paid off her debt to the bank yet – he received a handbag in the face for this news. But Coco was also in a rage with herself for not understanding the basic economics behind her business. The very next day she went back to work, determined to take her finances into her own hands, and make her fortune. By the following year she'd paid off her bill.

Coco's genius lay in breaking the rules and turning fashion formality on its head. At heart she was a rebel, set on freeing women from the constraints of corsetry. 'I wanted to give a woman comfortable clothes that would flow with her body. A woman is closest to being naked when she is well-dressed,' she later said, in a statement brilliant for its bitchin' blend of radicalism and sex. She used pedestrian fabrics and transformed them into pure luxury, and took notes from men's tailoring to create her now iconic collarless suits. She inspired women to wear their hair short, and she reclaimed the colour black from its association with mourning and funerals; her little black dress redefined the concept of chic.

Coco expanded her brand beyond her fashion house, to textiles, jewellery and accessories, using the now famous embracing CC of her initials to give each piece the stamp of authority. And then, in 1921, came Chanel No. 5. With Ernest Beaux, master perfumer, Coco set out to create a new fragrance. Legend has it that No. 5 was the result of a lab mistake. Coco was transfixed. It was an instant hit, and Chanel could not keep up with demand. Coco originally signed a deal with the Wertheimer brothers to market and produce it in return for 70 per cent of the profits, with the lucky chap who introduced them also taking a 20 per cent finder's fee, meaning Coco only pocketed 10 per cent. After decades of wrangling she won a better settlement and share of global sales. The bottle remains a design classic: simple, unfussy and bold, and today it's said a flacon of Coco's juice is sold every thirty seconds.

Coco's love life was as provocative as her approach to design. She never married, but had many high-profile affairs, with Igor Stravinsky, the poet Pierre Reverdy, the designer Paul Iribe and the Duke of Westminster among others, but it was her liaison with dashing German Hans Günther von Dincklage that would damage her reputation. Coco lived at the Ritz in Paris (of course she did) and during the Nazi occupation she used her connection with von D. to keep her pad there. She was heavily criticised for this, and for closing her business at the start of the war. She took herself off to Switzerland at the end of the war in 1945 to escape the acrimony.

In 1954 Coco staged a comeback – some said in response to Christian Dior's restrictive 'New Look', of which she was not a fan, saying: 'there are too many men in this business, and they don't know how to make clothes for women'. This time round she mined the rich seam of Hollywood, dressing the stars. She died while working on a new collection, at the age of eighty-seven, in her room at the Ritz.

This is a woman born in the nineteenth century who remains ice-queen cool even now in the twenty-first. She built a business empire in her own name from scratch, which lives on as one of the most iconic, most lusted-after brands ever invented. And she did it all in a time when being a woman was a massive hindrance. She fought like a tiger to protect and grow her assets, and she was brave, totally original, loyal to her friends and happy to call out people she thought were phonies. She took no shit whatsoever. It's a pretty *superbe* business model. *Chapeau, Coco!*

Nell Gwyn
and
Being Shameless

(1650–1687)

It's not easy being the bit on the side. Obviously, there's the ethical issue to wrestle with, and the full beam of other people's judgement. But beyond that, in between the sexy minibreaks, excitingly furtive hook-ups and the joy of only ever being seen in your best undies, it can be a lonely road, not having your beloved's full attention. And then there are fears about the future. Are you a soulmate, a fling or an exit strategy? Is he really going to leave his wife? Do you want him to? In some ways Nell Gwyn had had it good; a lot of this angsting simply didn't apply. The moral universe of King Charles II's court was unique, and Nell certainly thrived in it.

Eleanor Gwyn's origins are not 100 per cent clear but it is thought that she was born and raised in London's Covent Garden, the daughter of a father who came a cropper in debtor's prison and a mother who ran a brothel. As a teenager Nell got a gig hawking oranges at what is now the Theatre Royal in Drury Lane. These were exciting times in thespian circles as the theatres had only recently reopened, having been shut down by that buzzkill Oliver Cromwell until the Restoration in 1660. The happily reinstated King even went so far as to allow women to appear on stage for the first time. This opened the stage door for Nell in 1665. She blossomed into the best comic actress of her day, excellent at singing and dancing and reviewed by Samuel Pepys as 'pretty, witty Nell'. (Gallant Sam also called her a 'bold, merry slut'.) She starred in plays by the likes of Dryden and was also admired by such greats as Aphra Behn and the Earl of Rochester. She had three beaus called Charles but it was her third, King Charles II, who ensured her lasting fame. She met the King in 1669 and efficiently gave birth to his son in 1670, retiring from the theatre the next year.

Chas set Nell up in a house in Pall Mall, and, after he heard her summon their six-year-old son with the command 'Come here, you little bastard', His Majesty was moved to acknowledge the child (and his little brother) and made him Earl of Burford. Shrewd Nell was respected for not placing too many demands on the King: a sensible approach when you aren't the main marital dish. She was popular and gained the reputation of being the least greedy of his mistresses. For Nell was not the only woman in Charles's life. In fact, Charles's missus, poor old Catherine of Braganza, was far from Nell's main rival and the two apparently got on well. There was no question of the Merry Monarch leaving Catherine – over the course of their twenty-three-year marriage he refused to bow to pressure to divorce her even though they didn't have any children together and she was at one point accused of rallying a Catholic plot against him. Rule One of Affair Club: they never leave their wife.

Dryden described the King's comeback as a 'laughing, quaffing, unthinking time', and Charles certainly had his fun between the sheets – he had at least fourteen children with his circa thirteen mistresses. When she first hooked up with the King, Nell saw off another actress who was giving him the eye by apparently slipping laxatives into her food just before one of their dates. However, Nell's initial rival was Barbara Villiers, Duchess of Cleveland, a divisive, pushy figure at court, who even managed to rub the usually docile Queen up the wrong way. Babs had been the number one squeeze but was falling out of favour by the time Charles met Nell, and while Nellie became his bit of rough, he filled his aristocratic mistress vacancy with Louise de Kéroualle, Duchess of Portsmouth, who was probably a French spy. Louise's political interfering certainly proved unpopular at court, and Nellie enjoyed winding her up at every opportunity, ribbing her and calling her the 'weeping willow' for her emotional outbursts. Louise apparently returned fire by saying, 'anybody may know she has been an orange-wench by her swearing'. However, the pair of them also enjoyed taking tea together and playing cards, so it wasn't all handbags at dawn.

Nell and Charles kept the romance alive until the King's death in 1685, when famously his dying words to his brother, the soon-to-be James II, were to beg him not to let 'poor Nellie starve'. King James sorted Nell out financially and she lived comfortably until her own death from a stroke at the tender age of thirty-seven. She was buried under the altar of St Martin-in-the-Fields church thanks to her friendship with the vicar there.

So what made Nell such an excellent inamorata? Shamelessness. She didn't care what people said about her or about fulfilling respectable feminine ideals. She appears to have been a loyal friend to those who helped her and she was clearly a fun-loving, upbeat soul, who knew how to enjoy herself – particularly zooming around in her sedan chair, buying herself lovely things like a silver bed with the King's face carved into it, and stuffing herself with oysters and macaroons. She was also unashamed of the realities of her role – referring to herself to an angry crowd of people who had mistaken her for Louise as 'the *Protestant* whore' (as opposed to Louise, who was the Catholic one), to a cheery response. The best lesson we can learn from naughty Nell is to never be ashamed of where we come from or what we are, and to make the best of every situation we find ourselves in.

Rosalind Franklin
and
Being Difficult

(1920–1958)

It's interesting, isn't it, how being difficult is only a character fault if you have a vagina. We don't worry about Alfred Hitchcock's social skills, or whether John McEnroe was polite while he was smashing it all the way to the top. Difficult men, in fact, are celebrated in our culture – just think of James Bond or Batman as archetypes: granite-faced, saving the world and really not giving one about being nice. But for women, prickliness is judged more harshly; difficult women are passed over for not being 'team players' or having substandard 'diplomatic skills'. Just look at what nearly happened to champion chemist and DNA pioneer Rosalind Franklin.

Born in London, Rosalind was the second of five children. Her wealthy, Anglo-Jewish parents encouraged their children to speak their minds; they were fond of a political debate round the dinner table rather than a mild chat about the weather. From an early age, Rosalind's impressive intellect showed – her aunt called her 'alarmingly clever' – and she went on to study chemistry at Cambridge. After World War II she took a research job in Paris working under Jacques Mering, a brilliant X-ray crystallographer, whose breakthrough lay in applying imaging to mol-, ecules, revealing their density and structure. She had a fab time in gay Paree, developing an (unrequited) pash on Mering and taking herself off hiking in the Alps whenever she got a chance.

In 1951 she was hired to join a research team at King's College, London, working to uncover the structure of DNA. These were heady times in the world of science; two groups were working and competing with each other in the race to crack the secrets of our genetic code. Francis Crick and James Watson were based in Cambridge, and Maurice Wilkins and Rosalind in London. The relationship between Wilkins and our Rosalind was tense from the off: Wilkins regarded her as a member of his team, Franklin had been led to believe she would be working independently. They were mismatched personality-wise as well; Wilkins was shy, quiet and conflict-averse, Rosalind was punchy and confrontational. She became increasingly isolated in the poisonous atmosphere of the lab, but still managed to figure out that there were two types of DNA – wet and dry – and that the wet one would produce a much sharper X-ray image.

Over in Cambridge, Watson and Crick weren't having much luck, and in 1952 they were told by the head of their lab to give up their efforts, after complaints from King's that they were treading on toes. But when word got out that an American group was sniffing around the subject, they were put back on the case.

Watson made a trip to King's, and Wilkins showed him one of Rosalind's super-sharp X-ray photographs – the famous Photo 51 – which revealed the double helix shape.

Working on her own, Franklin had made amazing progress – she had figured out the double helix structure of DNA strands, and that the sequence of the bases on each strand might explain the 'biological specificity of DNA'. This was the Holy Grail of DNA investigations, and Rosalind came tantalisingly close to figuring it all out. In March 1953 she was invited to Cambridge with Wilkins to see the model that Watson and Crick had created using her data, and immediately recognised that it was correct. They all agreed that their findings would be published as the work of Watson and Crick, and the supporting data under Wilkins's and Franklin's separate names. Rosalind died at the age of thirty-seven of ovarian cancer, four years before the Nobel prize was awarded to Watson, Crick and Wilkins in 1962 and the reason for her exclusion from the prize is still debated today. None of the men acknowledged her in their acceptance speeches.

Ten years later Watson published a book about their discovery, and included a nasty takedown of Rosalind. He called out her frumpy clothes, lack of lippy and intense staring. Keep your make-over daydreams to yourself, Dr Watson. Throughout the book he insisted on calling her Rosy, which would have really stung since Rosalind was not a fan of the diminutive. In the rather apologetic epilogue he did manage to acknowledge her vital contribution and how hard it must have been for her, as a woman in science in those times. *The Double Helix* was an enormous success, but it rather backfired for Watson, as people began to dig a little deeper into how pivotal Rosalind's work had been. Today, she is celebrated as a true pioneer; countless academic institutes carry her name, her picture hangs in London's National Portrait Gallery alongside Crick, Watson and Wilkins, and Nicole Kidman starred in a play about her life.

So what's the lesson we can draw from Rosalind's tough experiences? True, she was not recognised within her lifetime but history's a bitch and the truth is hard to smother. Don't be afraid of being difficult – it's hard to do anything new without challenging the status quo and ruffling some feathers. Let's try a bit of reframing instead – you're not sulky, you are an outlier, a visionary, a maverick. So what if you're a little hard to get along with – cry me a river, people. Never feel that you have to stifle yourself with niceness. Celebrate those complexities, love your lonerdom and march to the beat of your very own drum.

Empress Dowager Cixi
and
Bossing It

(1835–1908)

Leaders are not born: they are forged in the fire of experience! We've all seen the motivational posters. It seems like everyone is supposed to be a leader these days: soon there will just be leaders leading leaders in an endless cycle of inspirational authority. Still, as you ascend the career ladder it's useful to know a bit about how to occupy your more senior role with confidence and pizzazz. There are assorted styles of management to choose from: the laissez-faire leader who delegates like a demon so they have time for their online shopping; the terrifying autocrat who shouts at the photocopier and whose power is absolute; the buddy-buddy democrat who wants to know all about your latest break-up. All well and good, but lady bosses beware: as a senior person with a set of ovaries and a seat of power, you're likely to have to fend off criticism however you decide to rule. Laissez-faire ladies are often accused of lacking commitment (particularly if they have kids); autocrats get labelled the boss bitch; and democrats, well, there's always the snowflake stamp swirling around.

Historians have viewed Empress Dowager Cixi of China's leadership style with ambivalence. Some have her down as a ruthless ruler, the Wicked Witch of the East, a terrorising Lady Macbeth figure. (She does seem to have been fond of the occasional well-timed use of poison.) Others view her as a single-minded, determined moderniser who saw off several assassination attempts and power struggles, and understood that compromise was the key to protecting her crumbling dynasty as the twentieth century approached.

Born to an ordinary family, Cixi was selected to join the Xianfeng emperor's girl gang inside the Forbidden City at the age of sixteen. To our eyes, underage concubines are not a good look, but at the time this was a plum job with access to a world of unimaginable wealth. (Think Rich Kids of Instagram without the freedom and the champagne.) She started out as a low-grade concubine (there were several strata), but was bumped up the pecking order when she produced a bouncing baby boy, Zaichun, who would go on to become Tongzhi emperor, in 1856. The Xianfeng emperor was in a tight spot at this point: he had the Taiping rebellion on one side, annoying Western powers sparking off the Opium Wars on the other, and not a lot of cash in the bank. When Cixi started piping up with her opinion on political matters, he freaked out and set up a council to prevent her ruling in the event of his death. But after he carked it at the age of thirty, Cixi seized the throne in a coup with her best friend, Empress Ci'an, Xianfeng's chief consort. They installed themselves as the supergroup

Empress Dowager Cixi and Empress Dowager Ci'an, until Cixi's son came of age.

As a chief, it's good to keep a bit of an aura of mystery around you. You could try shaking things up by emulating Cixi's method of presiding over her empire from behind a screen, since in the highly ritualised Chinese court it wasn't considered proper for ministers to look at her face. She didn't get out much; she couldn't have a chauffeur because he would have been required to genuflect whilst at the wheel – not a simple mirror, signal, manoeuvre. Despite these obstacles, Cixi managed to achieve peace and financial security: which the Emperor before her had failed to do. She saw that to survive, China needed to modernise, whilst protecting its culture from Westernising influences.

Annoyingly for Cixi, when Tongzhi came of age in 1861, she had to step back. (It's a sad truth of office life that occasionally you find yourself reporting to someone who used to bring you coffee.) However, Tongzhi wasn't up to the job by all accounts, and when he died in 1875, killed by smallpox (whisper it, did his mum knock him off?), Cixi seized power again, installing her three-year-old nephew Guangxu as the new Emperor-in-waiting. She adopted him, securing her position, and apparently forced him to address her as Heavenly Father. Bold.

Cixi's co-Empress Ci'an died in 1881 (again there are rumours that Cixi poisoned her, but it was likely a stroke) and nine years later Guangxu took the throne. He introduced a series of quite progressive reforms – cue tension and intrigue between aunt and nephew.

Cixi managed to put Guangxu under permanent house arrest after uncovering plots against her. She then went on to support the Boxer Rebellion in 1901, an anti-foreign peasant revolt, which ended in a crushing defeat for China by Japanese, Russian and European colonial powers. Shortly after this she issued her 'decree of self-reproach', blaming herself for a bad judgement call (good leaders know when to admit they've made a mistake) and saying that China should embrace the best of foreigners' ways (good leaders always make sure their strategy is flexible). After this Cixi instituted a programme of reforms: she gave a bit more freedom to the press, banned foot-binding and announced that China would be a constitutional monarchy with elections. Cixi died in 1908, one day after despatching Guangxu, who was seen off by acute arsenic poisoning. It's said she eliminated him for fear of her legacy being messed with after she'd gone. She named the two-year-old Puyi as her successor, who went on to become the last Emperor of China.

Cixi was buried in a blinged-up gold-leaf tomb of her own design, in control right to the end.

Was she a dictatorial despot who ran the illustrious Qing Empire into the ground and turned to murder when anyone looked at her funny? Or was she a visionary chief, determined to protect her legacy at any cost? Very few prominent leaders escape the limelight with an irreproachable reputation. Whatever side you fall on, there's no denying Cixi's endurance was deeply impressive. For nearly fifty years she kept her vice-like grip on power, and let's not forget she was not born into royalty; she took her opportunities, stepped up, leaned in and led from the front through huge political upheaval, all in a time when royal women couldn't even show their faces. As she said: 'Although I have heard much about Queen Victoria, I do not think her life is half as interesting and eventful as mine.'

Caroline Haslett
and
Giving Up Housework

(1895–1957)

You get home from work, switch on the lights, boil the kettle, stick on the dishwasher and run a load of laundry. If you're especially energised you might do a bit of ironing in front of *Big Little Lies*. All of this probably takes you an hour. Pre-1930 you'd be looking at *a whole day* spent just on the laundry, including several aggravating hours heating the stove up in the first place. It's no wonder feminism kicked off when this was the shape of a housewife's life, and it could take her ages just to make herself a cup of tea to mitigate the soul-destroying imprisonment in her grubby, smoky, damp shithole of a home, lacking even telly to distract her from the relentless drudgery that would dog every one of her days up to her inescapable, hobble-handed, grease-streaked death . . . OK, so perhaps we're overdoing it a bit, but we take the electrification of our homes so much for granted these days that a little corrective is surely in order.

Caroline Haslett was born in Sussex, into a close and religious family. Her father was an engineer and her mother was keen for her daughter to succeed in the world. Caroline wasn't really feeling the level of labour involved in running a house, sighing at the 'heavy starching and ironing, sweeping scrubbing polishing and dusting, all done by hand. I did not want to spend my life like that. It seemed a waste of time.' We hear you. She was equally lame at the needlework and cookery classes the girls endured at school, preferring botany and tinkering with her father's tools. Of her childhood, she said: 'I always believed in women, and when I was young I thought I had a mission to help to clear up the silly prejudice against them . . . In addition I had a great love of engineering. How wonderful it would be . . . to weld the two and open up the world of engineering to women!'

After school Caroline embarked on her plan. Getting the secretarial qualification that was the best available step for ambitious young women who wanted a career in business in the 1910s, she started work at the Cochran Boiler Company in 1914. By the time World War I arrived in the same year, Caroline was managing the London office and had designed her own boiler plans.

The shortage of labour during the war meant that women filled male roles in the workplace for the first time, but when peace was declared the returning soldiers reclaimed their jobs and the ladies were supposed to go back to their crochet. Not Caroline. In 1919 she saw an ad in *Engineering* magazine, reading: 'Required, Lady with some experience in Engineering Works, as Organising Secretary for a Women's Engineering Society'. This became the first of many illustrious appointments and she went on to become the Society's Director in 1941. She also co-founded the Electrical Association for Women, was Chairman of the Council of Scientific Management in the Home, was the first woman selected to join the Institute of Electrical Engineers in 1932 and the first woman Vice President of the Royal Society for the Prevention of Accidents, Chairman of the Hosiery Working Party (this sounds superfun) and Honorary Adviser on Women's Training to the Ministry of Labour. To add some initials into the mix she was also a JP, CBE and later DBE (and YGG, G9, PDH, TCOB*). Impressive stuff.

Caroline's purpose in all her roles was to make life better for women, both in and out of the home. She knew electricity was the key to freeing up women's time and adding respect and professionalism to domestic jobs: making them managers rather than dogsbodies. One of the coolest projects she was involved in was the All Electric House near Bristol, a brilliantly hip modernist home commissioned in 1935. It included an electric cooker, refrigerator, lights, fans, fires, heating, clocks, drying room, towel rail and power points. The idea was that the lady of the house would 'not have to carry wood and coal, clean dirty grates with the resultant dust on floors and furnishings,

* You Go Girl!, Genius!, Pretty Damn Hot!, Takin' Care of Business!

wind any clocks [that relentless clock-winding must have been a real drag], clean any metal used in the construction, buy any material for pelmets, clean windows frequently or have any chimney swept, and her cleaning, washing and decorating bills will correspondingly diminish'.

We all owe Caroline, and her colleagues, a big thank you for politicising and agitating for domestic electrification, liberating us from pelmet-stitching fatigue, and for her work in getting women into engineering jobs. She did all this without being a showboater, but as a quiet yet authoritative professional in an immaculate demi-wave and pearls. During the 1930s Caroline often went on the road, lecturing, advising and meeting the good and the great like Albert Einstein and Henry Ford. When World War II came, she advised on plans for the electrification of Great Britain, particularly contributing to the development of the safety plugs we have today which have shutters to stop small children electrocuting themselves.

This war again saw an influx of women into conventionally male disciplines, and since then education in technical subjects has opened up to women, although given that only 11 per cent of the engineering workforce in the UK today is female, it's clear Caroline's torch still needs bearing. Her motto was the brilliantly sensible and concise 'Get things done'. She helped women step out of the kitchen and get the boring things done much more quickly, so we can devote ourselves to the fun stuff. Take her example one step further and emancipate yourself from your remaining drudgery. Look carefully at where you spend your time. Who gives a damn if the floor needs hoovering or there's limescale on the shower taps – isn't there something more useful you could be doing? Like studying for an engineering degree so you can start a technological revolution to further emancipate your sisters, for example.

Amelia Earhart
and
Keeping your Own Name

(1897–disappeared 1937)

What's in a name? Well, quite a lot, actually. In medieval England, surnames usually defined what you did or what you were like – Butcher, Baker and Bigge. The Norman Conquest introduced hereditary surnames as well as the notion of coverture, a legal principle in which the wife essentially became the husband's property at the point of marriage and therefore took his name. Later, though, around the sixteenth century, the taking of your husband's name took on rather fluffier connotations derived from the Bible, to do with unity and being a team. In the seventeenth century, women started to campaign for the right to have the choice to keep their maiden name. Nowadays it's estimated that 75 per cent of women still take their husband's name when they slip on the ring, citing romance and the desire to share any offspring's appellation. It's a compelling argument – just think where Brand Beckham would be without it. After all, if it's a choice between your father's or your husband's cognomen, many women will choose the man they chose. But if you can't quite bring yourself to become Mrs Mangina and you're trying to explain to your future mother-in-law why you're not going to join the clan, there are plenty of inspiring women to light your way. Mary Wollstonecraft (see p. 13) kept hers and nineteenth-century suffragist Lucy Stone kept hers (and posthumously lent her handle to a society of women dedicated to preserving their names, the Lucy Stone League). But there's one stand-out sister who challenged preconceived ideas of what a woman could do, be or be called, throughout her entire life: awe-inspiring aviator Amelia Earhart.

Born at her grandmother's home in a small town in Kansas, Amelia spent a peaceful childhood there while her parents worked in Kansas City. Her father was an alcoholic; some say it was because she could never rely on him that she learned to be so self-sufficient. She was a tomboy as a child and loved to take ballsy physical risks. She also loved tinkering with mechanics. At an air show in 1920, she had her first go in a biplane and was instantly hooked, and by working as an office assistant, photographer and lorry driver, and with a cash injection from the Bank of Mum (not Dad), Earhart eventually bought her own plane, a bright-yellow bird which she called 'The Canary'. She also got a natty leather jacket and cut her hair to look the part.

But it was only after George P. Putnam – flamboyant publisher and PR guy – asked her if she would like to be the first woman to fly across the Atlantic that she saw she could make a living out of her obsession. Although she didn't actually lay a finger on the controls on that vapour-trailblazing crossing, she gained instant celebrity when Putnam published her book about her experience. After rejecting his marriage proposals an impressive five times, she finally said yes to Putnam on the sixth, and they embarked on an alliance that she described as a 'partnership with dual control'. But having launched Brand Amelia Earhart, she kept her own name. Amelia was incredibly cool and driven and she single-handedly set a series of aviation records: for altitude, fastest non-stop flight by a woman, first person to fly solo across the Pacific, first person to fly solo from Honolulu to Oakland . . . The list goes on. She also launched her own decidedly unfrilly fashion line and she was a tireless campaigner for women's rights: 'Women, like men, should try to do the impossible. And when they fail, their failure should be a challenge to others.'

As her fortieth birthday loomed, Amelia took on her midlife crisis with characteristic gusto, and set herself a new challenge: to fly around the world. With navigator Fred Noonan, she set out in her specially modified twin-engine Lockheed Electra. They had completed nearly two-thirds of the voyage when their plane disappeared halfway between Hawaii and Australia. They were never seen again. Rumours still swirl today as to what happened to Amelia and Fred.

Did bad weather confuse their navigation? Was her trip actually an espionage exercise and did she end up being captured by the Japanese? Did she land on a nearby island and survive for some time? Was she fed up with the trappings of celebrity and did she stage her own death so she could return to the US to live a quieter life under a different name? Of all of these, the last makes the *least* sense to us – Amelia Earhart was rightly proud of her incredible achievements, and more than happy to put her very own name to them. So if you choose to keep your own name, be proud of your own identity, and refer to the heroines of the past who refused, like Amelia, to succumb to pressure to conform. And remember: in many countries across the world, such as Spain, Holland and Chile, it would be considered positively outlandish to take your husband's name. And in Quebec and Greece it is against the law.

Sacagawea
and
Not Letting Anything Hold You Back

(c. 1788–c. 1812)

Most of the women in this book lived in times when there was no reproductive choice. If they didn't pop out some progeny, their husbands and neighbours were liable to get all judgy (despite the fact that childbirth always carried the risk of everyone involved dying). The choices we have today – whether we decide to have kids or not – are an incredible gift (see Marie Stopes on p. 135).

Dealing with the endless crying or the assault on your sense of self that is Baby Singalong time, it's very easy to see why some women decide against procreation. Once-proud Amazons now find themselves limping through life hobbled by changing bags, speaking gibberish to an entity with less intelligence than a dolphin, and wondering who they are now that they don't see their friends any more. Pregnancy, birth and looking after young children can easily make a gal feel fragile, frustrated and trapped, but there is an exceptional role model to show that this needn't be the case in the interpreter and explorer Sacagawea.

Born into the Native American Shoshone tribe, Sacagawea lived a life that has passed into legend. She was the daughter of a chief but was stolen from her family by an enemy tribe, the Hidatsa, and sold to be the extra wife of a French-Canadian trapper. The melodiously named Toussaint Charbonneau had the incommodious reputation of being a right stinker: 'a man of no peculiar merit' and an attempted rapist, according to reports from the time. There are no records of what Sacagawea thought of her husband.

In November 1804, President Jefferson's military expedition to explore the uncolonised far west of the continent arrived in the Charbonneaus' village. This troop was also known by a grandiose name, the Corps of Discovery – neglecting to notice, as was the fashion in those days, that the area they were 'discovering' had already been found some time earlier by the tribes of the native population. The Corps was led by Captain Meriwether Lewis and Lieutenant William Clark, who were keen to find interpreters to help them as they made their journey further up the Missouri River and into uncharted, potentially deadly territory.

Charbonneau and Sacagawea between them could speak French, Hidatsa and Shoshone, and they were soon employed by the Corps even though Sacagawea was heavily pregnant with their first child. The expedition holed up for the winter and, in February 1805, Sacagawea gave birth to a son, Jean Baptiste. Lewis had some medical abilities and assisted with the birth, which he described, discerningly, as 'tedious and the pain violent', until they gave Sacagawea a tincture of rattlesnake tail to speed things up. When

Jean Baptiste was just two months old, the thirty-three-person expedition set off, with the indomitable seventeen-year-old Sacagawea – the only woman – carrying her baby on her back. They went on to travel all the way to the Pacific, mainly by boat, with Sacagawea contributing her knowledge of foraging, passable routes and clothes-making. She even jumped in and rescued vital supplies and equipment from a river when her panicky husband nearly capsized their canoe.

When the party reached the Rocky Mountains, the boats were clearly no longer an option (probably a relief for Charbonneau, whom Lewis, in a scathing burn, called 'the most timid waterman in the world'), and they had to negotiate with the local Shoshone for horses. By amazing coincidence, they ran into Sacagawea's long-lost brother, who helped them at this crucial moment.

The journey was tough going, beset by illness and the threat of attack by hostile locals or grizzly bears, and one man died. Sacagawea made it all the way to the Pacific and then all the way back to St Louis again – some 6,400 kilometres – gaining the respect and friendship of Clark in particular, who offered to educate Jean Baptiste when he got older: 'As to your little Son (my boy Pomp) you well know my fondness for him.' After Sacagawea's death, thought to be from fever in 1812, Clark did indeed look after both 'Pomp' and the Charbonneaus' baby daughter, Lisette.

Doing her thing in a riot of intersectionality – as a non-white teen mom – it's hard to find a better example than Sacagawea of an unstoppable, gutsy heroine to pep up your spirits and make you believe that anything is possible. Her story certainly makes the thought of having to wrestle a screaming infant into a car seat to get to Sainsbury's seem far more manageable. And best of all, although her feats are heightened by the fact that she achieved them while a new mother, motherhood is not what defined her. The expedition helped the mapping of the west and the eventual expansion of the United States into this area, and Sacagawea was a key player in its success. Stupendously brave and admirable, an expert linguist, forager and all-round heroine, Sacagawea is honoured around the world for her achievements in this unique endeavour, alongside the men she travelled with.

Clara Schumann
and
Being Savvy with Your Cash

(1819–1896)

Prodigious pianist Clara Schumann has the mixed fortune of being synonymous with two famous musical men: her husband, the composer Robert Schumann, and her BFF Johannes Brahms. Add a dominating and nutty father into the mix, and the result is that much of what we know about her is seen through the prism of the men in her life. However, Clara was an important figure in musical history in her own right, and ended up more in charge of her own destiny – and money – than any of the fellows around her.

Little Clara Wieck was born in Leipzig. Her parents divorced when she was six because of her mother's philandering and, given his automatic custody rights, Clara found herself the focus of her ambitious piano-teacher father's attention. She studied hard and was tremendously gifted, although since she didn't speak a word until she was four, people originally assumed she was deaf.

The pint-sized pianist gave her first solo concert in Leipzig in 1830 (where she played two of her own compositions) and went on tour drumming up business for her dad and bringing home the notes. Her family also invited a new lodger – Robert Schumann – to study with her father. Just like popstars who give private concerts today, Clara could put on a VIP show and in 1831 she played for the famous writer Goethe, who supplied her with a booster cushion so she could reach the keyboard.

By 1837 Clara was an established prodigy – when she played for the Emperor in Vienna he dubbed her 'Wundermädchen'* – and she and Robert were in love. Inconveniently, Clara's dad thought Bobby was a no-hoper, so whisked her off to Dresden on tour again to keep them apart. However, just as her playing rejected the demure and decorative tinkling expected of women at this time, defiant Clara refused to obediently kick Robert to the kerb. In 1839, having stayed in touch in secret, they decided to get hitched. Clara's father refused to give his consent until a nigh-year-long legal suit from Robert forced him to, and even then he declined to pass over her hard-earned concert earnings. One happy outcome from this feud was that Clara renewed her relationship with her estranged mother. The couple had eight children together but Clara still promoted her husband's work, toured, composed and taught, especially as Robert's mental health and ability to work became increasingly unstable.

In 1853 the Schumanns became friends and champions of young Johannes Brahms – a relationship

* Wondergirl.

that grew into an intense bond between Clara and JB, although historians don't believe they ever did the dirty. In 1854 Robert attempted suicide and then admitted himself to a mental hospital because he was worried he would hurt his wife. Clara was not allowed to visit him until just before his death in 1856. During this time, Clara relied on support from her close friends, including her muso pals Jenny Lind and the violinist Joseph Joachim. Brahms helped her run her household, but they separated after Robert died.

Finding herself a single mother with seven surviving children to support, the Queen of the Piano employed nannies and began touring again, which she continued to do for the next forty years. She was a demon for the paperwork, carefully keeping a record of all her contracts and itineraries. She dealt with the financial fragility of her position as a widow by making damned sure she could be counted on for her family's income. In 1878 she became an influential teacher at the Hoch Conservatory in Frankfurt, where she taught right up until her death from a stroke in 1896.

As well as being one of the superstars of the nineteenth-century music scene, Clara composed many admired pieces, such as 'Quatre Polonaises pour le pianoforte' (1831), 'Piano Trio in G minor Op. 17' (1846), and the chamber work 'Drei Romanzen für

Pianoforte' (1855). She gave up composing in later life after she began to suffer from Impostor Syndrome (see Isabella Beeton on p. 147). Nothing encapsulates the sorry state of expectations and support for women at this point like her very sad statement: 'I once believed that I possessed creative talent, but I have given up this idea; a woman must not desire to compose – there has never yet been one able to do it. Should I expect to be the one? There is nothing that surpasses the joy of creation.' (See Enheduanna on p. 277 to counteract this bleak assessment.) Clara became a shrewd businesswoman and expertly managed extensive domestic duties, all the while excelling in a typically male field. And in her case, as in most modern women's, domestic duties didn't just mean shopping and cleaning while waiting for hubby to top up the housekeeping jar: Clara took financial responsibility for herself and her children.

Make sure you know your dough – it's part of adulting not to be romantically broke all the time. It's fair enough to want to treat yourself to a pick-me-up present after a bad day, but you've got to know exactly what's in your bank account before you splash the cash. Debt can very quickly spiral out of control, and control is exactly what you want when it comes to your finances. Get that overdraft authorised, save a little every month, always check for promotional vouchers when online shopping, congratulate yourself on your patience and self-denial when you don't buy those gorgeous shoes. Salaries, budgets, cutting up your credit cards: all of these things are definitely boring AF, but if Clara could manage this as an ivory-tickling teen then you can too.

Masako Katsura
and
Leaning In

(1913–1995)

There are some disciplines in which females aren't supposed to thrive: mowing lawns, building shelves, barbecuing, taking out bins, beating the shit out of people, sinking pints and all sport. However, since the day women threw their petticoats to the winds and started to wear trousers without being spat at in the street for upending civilisation (NB fewer than one hundred years ago) a shocking discovery has been made: women can do sport after all! And what's more they're pretty damned good at it.

It's depressing that women's sport is still considered a less exciting and commercially appealing sister to men's (see the perennial knicker-twist that recurs every Wimbledon). We still need to fix the cultural emphasis on boys being muscular and active, and girls being contrastingly valued for their fatty deposits and charming chitchat. However, there's no denying that there are plenty of astonishingly gifted and disciplined professional sportswomen out there in every category; just think of Althea (see p. 169), Mina (see p. 31), Serena, Tanni, Kelly, Ellen, Billie Jean, Marit, Nicola, Jackie, Laura, Tatiana, Ryu, Janica, Marta, Simone, Ellie, Sana, Luciana and Laura.*

---

* Gibson (tennis), Wylie (swimming), Williams (tennis), Grey-Thompson (athletics), Holmes (athletics), MacArthur (sailing), King (tennis), Bjorgen (skiing), Adams (boxing), Joyner-Kersee (athletics), Trott (cycling), Gutsu

However, disappointingly, searching for 'world's top sportswomen' is very likely to surface 'world's most beautiful sportswomen' near the top of your results, followed by 'world's sexiest sportswomen'. Needless to say the same search results do not arise for men, however sexy and beautiful they are.

Back in the 1950s female sporting heroes were thin on the (playing) ground(s), even for more sedate games like billiards where superior muscle mass doesn't give you an advantage. This is what made the career of Masako Katsura exceptional. Masako (later known by the nickname 'Katsy') was born in Tokyo. Her brother-in-law owned a billiards club, where she used to hang and where she eventually started working in her teens. In case you're thinking that billiards and the pool you play in your local pub are the same thing, they are similar in terms of skillset, but billiards has different variants, rules, numbers of balls and, crucially, no pockets in the table. Billiards used to be more of a thing back in the day, but now its cousins snooker and pool rule the roost (two of the many variations of cue games that developed from the original billiards which was played as early as the fifteenth century).

(gymnastics), So-yeon (golf), Kostelić (skiing), Vieira da Silva (football), Biles (gymnastics), Simmonds (swimming), Mir (cricket), Aymar (hockey), Langman (netball).

Masako honed her skills through practice, practice, practice (perhaps as an early adopter of the ten thousand-hour rule). The most famous quote attributed to her is: 'Men want to beat me. I play men, six, seven hours a day. Men no like, they do not beat me.'

Masako won her first tournament when she was fifteen. She attracted the attention of professional player Kinrey Matsuyama, who trained her, and she went on to become Japan's only female professional billiards player, coming second in the national championships three times. In 1950 Masako married an American, stationed in Japan as part of the post-war US force there. When he was recalled back to the States she went with him and began her US career by playing exhibition matches. When she was invited to play in the 1952 World Championship, she became the first woman anywhere to compete at this level in billiards. She came seventh, then fifth the next year and fourth the year after that, beating a lot of guys, and earning herself the title The First Lady of Billiards.

Masako did not manage to avoid the media scrutiny of her body that modern female athletes endure, even though she competed in formal clothing rather than any kind of revealing sportswear. Coverage of the time accentuated how tiny she was and typical newspaper articles referred to her as 'cute' and 'pert'. *Time* magazine began an article about her by describing how she was 'cue-tall (5 ft.) and light as chalk (96 lbs.)'. However, one of her fellow players described her in more competitive terms: 'The killer instinct – that broad had it, and never mind the little smile.' Although fetishised to some extent as a curiosity in the masculine world she inhabited, Masako was clearly an exceptional pool shark and she also wrote two books about her sport. She was aware of her position as a trailblazer: 'I hope my tour will convince women that billiards is not only a man's game. Women can play just as well as men.' So stop mooching about in your athleisurewear and find your sporting métier, whether it's billiards, boules, boxing, badminton or base jumping. And be sure to throw like a girl.

Enheduanna
and
Sparking Your Creativity

(c. 2300 BCE)

For many of us, the dream of finding the time to let our creative juices flow can feel tragically remote. Yes, we *know* it's crucial to find silence and space to allow for a mindful visit from the Muses, but it's more likely that after a day of work you'll find us slack-jawed in front of one more episode of *Love Island*. But if you can carve out some time to feed your inner imagineer, the rewards are huge, from making your job work better for you to easing relationship tensions and generally making yourself feel more alive and fulfilled. The power of innovation is invigorating and there's one woman we can turn to for inspiration who took it a step further – she didn't just revel in her creativity, she *owned* it. Living around 2300 BCE, High Priestess and Princess Enheduanna is the most ancient lady in our assemblage of badass bygone babes. She was the daughter of King Sargon I of Akkad, who appointed her High Priestess of the moon god Nanna and the goddess Inanna in the holy city of Ur (in present-day southern Iraq).

King Sargon declared himself ruler of southern Mesopotamia, uniting a number of city-states into an empire, including Ur. He installed his daughter there in the holiest job going, which helped him to bring divided cultures together and reassert his power by associating his reign with the deities. Enheduanna took her responsibility seriously, and must have been pretty good at her job: she remained in her post for over forty years, bagging herself the claim of being history's first writer – yes, the very first named writer in our planet's history, man or woman – along the way.

We know quite a lot about this ancient cleric because she left behind a truly remarkable creative legacy. Her body of work included forty-two hymns dedicated to temples across Mesopotamia and a series of poems, the most famous of which is 'The Exaltation of Inanna'. There is also the celebrated Disc of Enheduanna – not audio of her greatest hits but a depiction of her which shows us just how grand she was. Found in excavations in 1921 it shows Enheduanna partaking of a bit of ritual – she is captured with a bald and naked priest crouching in front of her, while she rocks some elegant robes, glorious braids and a very natty turban. This was a woman at the top of her game.

The poems and hymns give us even more of a sense of her character. Her 'Exaltation of Inanna' follows a proper narrative arc – we begin with effusive praise of her goddess's attributes, some terrifying, some beautiful, all awe-inspiring. Then Enheduanna mentions a political threat which has resulted in her exile, and asks for revenge: it's payback time. It ends on a triumphant note: she has revengineered her restoration to her rightful position as the holiest priestess. There are many amazing things in this poem – we particularly enjoyed this compliment: 'Mistress of heaven, with the great pectoral jewels' – but perhaps the most astonishing is her keen sense of authorship and ownership. The poems are political, passionate, complex, and more than anything they are Enheduanna's. She is the first recorded person to use the first person, in the lines 'I am Enheduanna' (eat your heart out, Moana). In 'I have given birth to this song for you', she describes the process of creativity in distinctly feminine terms. It's worth pausing to remember that she was doing all this about a millennium and a half before that guy was tackling the *Iliad* and the *Odyssey*.

Some have said that Enheduanna is the author of authorship itself – but if this feels a touch too lofty in terms of aspiration, note that the traits she displayed which we all associate with creative people are far more attainable. She was original, inventive, passionate, committed and fiery – all qualities we can adopt. Remember: you do not have to be in the business of laying down epic poetry or art built to last for millennia to ignite that creative spark. Everyday creativity is the thing to aim for. Ask more questions. Interrogate whether that recipe could be made even more delicious if you added some out-there ingredient. Re-arrange your furniture. Carve a Death Star pumpkin this Halloween (OK, this may also be out of reach but we saw one once and it was really cool).

Josephine Baker
and
Having It All

(1906–1975)

Women 'having it all' is a coded phrase for 'having what men have'. It usually refers to women trying to find true love and excel at their jobs at the same time, or mothers struggling to combine family life with work, as well as demanding standards of fitness, attractiveness, cultivation and sexual fulfilment.

The life of celebrated and adored exotic dancer, singer, mother, spy, war hero and activist Josephine Baker appears to tick all these boxes. But things didn't start so brilliantly for Freda Josephine McDonald, who was born in St Louis to a poor family. Her grandparents were freed slaves and her mother was an ex-dancer and laundress – her father hightailed off not long after Josephine was born. Even as a young child she had to miss school to work as a cleaner and nanny to help pay the bills, before ending up aged thirteen as a waitress in a club (where she also got married for a couple of weeks to a punter).

Josephine started dancing on the street and in clubs and, despite being called 'too dark and too skinny' early in her career, ended up joining a dance troupe, and marrying again at the age of fifteen. In 1921 she got a part in a touring production of the seminal black musical *Shuffle Along* and this set her on her path to Broadway. Four years later she was invited to join a show travelling to Paris to perform at the Théâtre des Champs-Elysées. This would prove to be her life-changing moment.

Paris in the 1920s was fascinated by the Harlem Renaissance, American jazz and primitivism, and Josephine's dance number required her to perform the *danse sauvage* wearing just a feather skirt. This fetishisation of African culture obviously feels wrong today, but Josephine grabbed her golden opportunity with both hands and revelled in amping it all up. She used to drive around in a Rolls-Royce with her pet cheetah and, once she'd moved to the prestigious Folies Bergère, took on the act that made her truly famous – a spirited twerking number wearing just a belt made of sparkling bananas. She was well aware of the difference between performance and reality: 'Since I personified the savage on the stage, I tried to be as civilised as possible in daily life.'

From this point on the Black Pearl was a sensation. She became the most highly paid entertainer in Europe, no mean feat for a black American woman. She received hundreds of marriage proposals, and was admired by Hemingway, Picasso, Frida Kahlo (see p. 85) and Colette. She also expanded her repertoire to include singing and appearing in films. Sadly her home country didn't take to her with the same enthusiasm when she returned to visit and she became a French citizen in 1937, and also married for the third time.

When World War II erupted Jo did not abandon her new country. She was a sub-lieutenant in the Women's Auxiliary Air Force and worked for the Resistance, smuggling secrets in her sheet music and underwear. After the war she was awarded the Croix de Guerre and was made a Chevalier of the Légion d'honneur. She married again in 1947 and bought a fifteenth-century château in the Dordogne. After painful and unsuccessful experiences trying to have a baby, Josephine eventually adopted twelve children. Beyond her wish to be a mother, she had a firm political purpose in her construction of her family. The children were all from different places, races and religions and she called them her 'Rainbow Tribe'. She essentially made her château into a kind of utopian theme park for visitors to see how people from diverse backgrounds could all get along. A laudable experiment but doubtless an extremely weird environment to grow up in.

As an extension of this vision of a healthy multi-racial and multicultural community, Josephine became active in the civil rights movement in the USA and worked with the NAACP (see Rosa Parks on p. 25) in the 1950s. After kicking up a stink at the swish Stork Club in Manhattan in 1951 when they refused to serve her, Josephine incurred the wrath of right-wingers, who labelled her a Commie troublemaker. One good thing to come out of this was that she gained a true pal in the young blonde actress who was so offended by the treatment Josephine received that she walked out of the Stork with her. Grace Kelly and Josephine's ensuing friendship lasted for the rest of Josephine's life.

In 1968 the expense of the chi-chi château sent Josephine bankrupt and her rainbow tribe was scattered between her, her family and her ex-husband: the by-now Princess Grace kindly furnishing her with a home in Monaco. But five years later she hit a professional high when she performed again in the US, at Carnegie Hall, to a rapturous reception. Not long after, in 1975, she staged a major show in Paris to celebrate the anniversary of her first performance there. It was a triumph but just a few days later the divine Ms Baker was found dead in her bed surrounded by her acclamatory reviews. Twenty thousand people lined the streets for her funeral and she was buried with military honours.

So did Josephine Baker have it all? She was undoubtedly an extraordinary woman, and the heights of fame and political influence she achieved are not within the reach of most of us. However, when pondering this tricky question of 'it all', remember that there are two ways of looking at Josephine's story:

was she a stripper with four failed marriages, rejected by her homeland, a bizarre mother most interested in her children for display purposes, a political loose cannon with enemies, a bankrupt who lost her home and aged in the spotlight? Or was she an astonishingly unique and powerful performer, a quick-witted woman who had close friendships and romantic relationships with many men and women, a brave defender of her adopted country, a civil rights champion, a well-meaning mother remembered fondly in the main by her children, a style icon (even in her later years in her marvellously massive sunglasses) whose influence is still felt today and who has inspired films and books and even Beyoncé? I think most of us would be immensely proud to have anything near the kind of life she had. But as the alternative versions attest, nobody gets it all right all the time. Having it all just means having what you want, on your own terms, to the best of your abilities: and the fabulous Baker girl certainly never stopped trying to do that.

Queen Victoria
and
Getting Over Loss

(1819–1901)

Psychiatrists have established that the process of picking yourself up after a loss goes through several stages. Let's take a break-up as an example. The stages are: 1. Shock ('!'); 2. Denial ('High maintenance?! Are you kidding me? I am not high maintenance, FFS'); 3. Anger ('It's not that common, it doesn't happen to every guy, and it is a big deal!'); 4. Pain and guilt ('I am. I am high maintenance. I never deserved a prince like you'); 5. Depression and loneliness ('I just feel so alone. Who will buy my cashmere pants now?') – btw, this is the phase where your friends tend to get bored and start checking their phones when you go through what his last text said for the zillionth time; and finally, 6. Acceptance ('I need to find my own way to cashmere pants') and engaging with life again ('Hey, maybe there's more to life than cashmere pants. And look, that hottie just swiped right for me #happydaysarehereagain'). But if you're lodged in the black fug of loss, there is one woman who was famous for giving good grief who can show us how to find our way through with style.

Look a little further beyond the image of Queen Victoria as a dowdy old lady, swathed perpetually in black, faced etched with lines of unimaginable pain, and a different story starts to emerge. Alexandrina, Victoria's mum, was the Duchess of Kent, and her dad was the fourth son of George III, making her fifth in line to the throne. But since her uncles were a bunch of old guys, and her dad died when she was a baby, her future as Queen looked pretty certain from the off. She was raised by her mother at Kensington Palace under the beady eye of her dad's former servant John Conroy, who by all accounts was a power-crazed upstart who saw Vicky as his ticket to the top. Conroy and the Duchess devised a dark plan called the Kensington System, designed to make the young royal utterly dependent on her mother: they kept her under sustained surveillance right into her teens, mum and daughter slept in the same room, she was not allowed to hang with other kids and a strict routine was adhered to at all times. When she finally hopped up onto the throne just after her eighteenth birthday, it's said that the first thing Victoria asked for was an hour on her own, a luxury she had never had.

Queen V. very quickly realised that her only escape from her mum and Conroy had to be a husband. She'd had crushes before, most notably on Lord Melbourne, her first Prime Minister, but when her dashing German cousin Prince Albert of Saxe-Coburg arrived on the scene with his luxuriant moustache, she had eyes for nobody else, and they got hitched in 1840. The couple were seriously hot for each other but also feisty: at four feet eleven inches Victoria may have been short of stature but she had a towering personality, and she didn't take at all kindly to Albert's attempts to muscle in on all that ruling she had to do. Also, Vicky really hated pregnancy and breastfeeding, and suffered badly from post-natal depression – despite this they went on to have nine children together, the first born a neat nine months after their wedding.

Whilst radicalism isn't quite what comes to mind when we think of V. and A., over their twenty-one years of marriage they shook up the image of the monarchy, taking an interest in social matters like child welfare and factory conditions, becoming patrons of many charities, and overseeing the Great Exhibition of 1851. Victoria leaned on her man in matters micro and macro – from which bonnet she should wear to diplomatic interventions with America. So when Albert died suddenly from typhoid at the age of forty-two, Victoria was poleaxed by grief. Official mourning was supposed to last two years, but she refused to appear in public for almost three – earning herself the nickname the 'widow of Windsor'. She kept Albert's rooms untouched and wore black for the rest of her life. As she retreated further and further from view the one thing that did rouse her interest was commissioning loads of public memorials for her angel. Oh, that and John Brown, her ghillie (like a hunting 'n fishing PA) at the Balmoral estate in Scotland. Their relationship set tongues a-wagging, and one biographer believes they may have had a marriage ceremony and even shared a bed (but it's unlikely they ever did the deed).

No one wants a dreary queen, and Victoria's retreat from public life caused public displeasure to brew; there were even calls for her abdication. Then, exactly ten years after Albert's death, their eldest son the Prince of Wales caught the same disease that had done for his papa. When he recovered, Victoria appeared on the balcony at Buckingham Palace after a thanksgiving service. All she had to do was wave and survive a well-timed assassination attempt and the public loved her all over again. She set her mind to marrying off her offspring around Europe. In later life she added Empress of India to her CV, and embarked on another intense relationship, this time with Abdul Karim, who was employed to teach her Urdu and how to eat a curry properly.

Queen Victoria died in January 1901 at the age of eighty-one, leaving instructions that she should be dressed in her wedding veil, and that Albert's dressing gown, along with, rather creepily, a plaster cast of his hand should be placed in her coffin, plus a picture of John Brown and some of his hair, and his mum's wedding ring, which he'd given to her.

So even though in many ways Queen Vic more than lived up to her rep as the mother of all mourners, it's clear she found some activities to help ease the pain. Give yourself as much time as you need to properly come to terms with your loss, whatever it is, but try not to make a career out of misery, however fabulous you look in black. Acknowledge your unhappiness and give it time; don't fight your feelings – Victoria was not one for a bright smile in the face of pain. One of the simplest lessons we can learn from her, which doesn't cost the Koh-i-Noor, is to get out in the fresh air. OK, you may not have fifty thousand acres of your own prime Scottish countryside in which to weep and wail, but a walk in your local park or by your nearest river will do you the world of good, we promise. And taking up with a younger lover is always going to prove a fun distraction, whatever the problem.

Mary Seacole
and
Ageing Disgracefully

(1805–1881)

Ageing is something we all have to face, but being an older woman has its own special indignities; as well as the universal corporeal slowdown, we also find ourselves ignored and pitied once our nubility and fertility have faded. Where men with their sexy salt-and-pepper hair are usually taken more seriously in their mature years, women are inclined to be judged as old bags, fussbuckets and battleaxes. One lady who refused to go gentle into that good night was spunky adventuring nurse Mary Seacole. As well as having a fierce sense of style (she liked to wear blinding colours and a set of unearned medals across her chest), Mary, a Jamaican-Scottish woman, had a bold and daring spirit. She travelled around the Caribbean with her husband, and continued to roam even after his death. She lived briefly in Panama with her half-brother and found herself nursing victims of a cholera epidemic there, using traditional medicine learned from her mother. She also ran a canteen and went on to use these experiences in Jamaica during a yellow fever outbreak, and then, most famously, in the last years of the Crimean War between 1855 and 1856.

At the fine age of fifty, Mary decided to fling herself into a new enterprise. She wanted to help the British war effort in the Crimea and applied to work there as a nurse. However, the War Office turned her down. Undeterred, she travelled instead to the port of Balaclava under her own steam. She set up a boarding house that sold food, drink and supplies, and her actions (and tea and sympathy) were so appreciated by the soldiers that, after the war, they set up a fund to support her back in London. She met, but did not work with, Florence Nightingale, who endorsed her with the excellent backhanded compliment that there was 'much kindness – also much drunkenness and improper conduct, wherever she is'.

Having returned to the UK, Mary was inspired by the Indian Rebellion in 1857 to offer her services once again, although again she was turned down. This same year she published her lively autobiography, *The Wonderful Adventures of Mrs. Seacole in Many Lands*. Mary died in 1881 and her grave was for some time lost, as was her reputation. Both have since been restored and you can visit her resting place at St Mary's Cemetery in Kensal Green, London, should you feel moved to pay your respects to this exceptional woman.

A true exemplar of get-up-and-go, despite some controversy over her actual medical qualifications, it is undeniable that Mary Seacole – nurse, hotelier, restaurateur, shopkeeper, patriot, adventurer, traveller, entrepreneur, cook and author – was an amazingly determined woman. She didn't let the prejudices she faced – as a middle-aged, mixed-race woman – hold her back in either her ambitions or her generosity of spirit. Perhaps jaunting off to a war zone in a foreign country is a step too far, but there's rarely a bad time to follow Mary's example of taking a risk and trying something new – even if it's more along the lines of developing an enthusiasm for yoga or French cinema.

Afterword

'We delight in the beauty of the butterfly, but rarely admit the changes it has gone through to achieve that beauty.'

Maya Angelou, writer and civil rights activist

We hope that you've found the stories in this book inspiring and useful. These fifty exceptional people found their moment of butterfly-brilliance at different ages, in vastly different circumstances and in different fields of expertise. We were struck by their struggles and their willingness to swim against the tide. They prove that it's possible to take on bad odds, bad families, bad cultural stereotypes and bad luck, and still make a difference. Very few of them were thrust into the limelight because of their birth but what unites them is that all of them worked hard to make their lives matter. And of course they weren't the only ones: it was a tough task to winnow our list down to just fifty. Where is Maya we hear you say? What about Marie Curie? Or Joan of Arc? Or Mother Teresa? It took us a long time to decide on our final cut. We wanted to make sure that we shone a light on some of the lesser-known heroines of history as well as focussing on the greats who have something to teach us about today's world.

Many of our fifty suffered outrageous treatment: they were slandered, assaulted, underestimated, side-lined and erased. None of them was perfect – some of them did terrible as well as wonderful things. They were morally complex people but we're here to celebrate their achievements rather than how 'nice' they were along the way. All of them triumphed despite living in far more savagely patriarchal circumstances than we endure today. We truly believe that things are getting better for women. But if there's one request we'd like to make of you, it is to talk about female achievements more; both from the past and today. Make sure what you contribute is acknowledged: tell your BFF what you admire about her; celebrate your work wife; campaign for statues for historical role models; call out misogyny whenever you see it. Women still need to muscle in on our public spaces and make much more noise.

The women in this book have often had backing from other broads – just think of Fanny and Mina, Grace and Josephine, Althea and Angela – relation-ships defined by cheerleading, support and love, which provided the bedrock for sisterly success. So what other lessons do we take from our ladies? Be generous with one another, celebrate each other's wins, but don't sweat the losses too much either – as Amazing Grace Hopper pointed out, fear of failure is the killer; it's the trying that counts. Our women didn't get everything right, and sometimes got a lot wrong, so don't beat yourself up about mistakes you make on your own path. It doesn't mean there won't be a book like this written about you someday.

And of course this is not just women's business. In the battle of the sexes none of us wants a combat zone littered with bloodied victims. Let's big up the boys too. After all, many of our women's fathers and husbands were instrumental in encouraging them to push beyond cultural expectations and desires. And many other men have helped the feminist cause through history: think of ex-slave Frederick Douglass's heroic efforts with abolition and women's suffrage in America; or French maths whizz, philosopher and revolutionary the Marquis de Condorcet's radical support for women's rights back in the 1700s; or even Mahatma Gandhi, who famously said: 'To call woman the weaker sex is a libel; it is man's injustice to woman.' We hear you, *Bapu*. So celebrate all these guys with your boyfriend, your dad and your brothers, and make sure your daughters as well as your sons know about them. Our fifty fabulous females show that the world becomes a richer place for everyone if women are allowed to fulfil their potential. It's up to all of us to futureproof our equality.

Sources

We have consulted a range of books, articles, obituaries, radio and TV programmes and websites in putting together this book. We particularly relied on our trusted friends the *Guardian*, *New York Times*, *History Today*, the BBC, the Smithsonian, *Telegraph*, *London Review of Books*, *The Times*, *Independent*, *The Atlantic*, *Washington Post*, *Japan Times* and the *Encyclopaedia Britannica* and the various museums, trusts and organisations that look after the legacies of these extraordinary women.

Readers who want to investigate further might be interested in the following:

The Celts by Alice Roberts, Heron Books, 2016.
A Vindication of the Rights of Women by Mary
     Wollstonecraft, Vintage, 2013.
*Romantic Outlaws: The Extraordinary Lives of Mary
     Wollstonecraft and Mary Shelley* by Charlotte Gordon,
     Hutchinson, 2015.
The Life and Death of Mary Wollstonecraft by Claire
     Tomalin, Weidenfeld and Nicolson, 1974.

Mae West: Great Interviews of the Twentieth Century by
   Charlotte Chandler, Guardian Books, 2007. (To start
   your film journey through Mae's work, we'd suggest:
   She Done Him Wrong, 1933. Directed by Lowell
   Sherman. *I'm No Angel*, 1933. Directed by Wesley
   Ruggles.)

Rosa Parks by Douglas Brinkley, Viking, 2000.

*Strength of Purpose: Australian Women of Achievement
   from Federation to the mid-Twentieth Century* by
   Susanna De Vries, HarperCollins, 1998. (There is also
   a wonderful audio interview with Mina Wylie by Neil
   Bennetts from 1975, to be found online at the National
   Library of Australia.)

Women Poets of Japan by Ikuku Atsumi and Kenneth
   Rexroth, New Directions, 1982.

*Embracing the Firebird: Yosano Akiko and the Rebirth of
   the Female Voice in Modern Japanese Poetry* by Janine
   Beichman, University of Hawaii Press, 2001.

*Feminism in Modern Japan: Citizenship, Embodiment and
   Sexuality* by Vera Mackie, Cambridge University Press,
   2003.

*The Enigma of the Age: The Strange Case of the Chevalier
   D'Éon* by Cynthia Cox, Longmans, 1966.

Granuaile: Ireland's Pirate Queen: Grace O'Malley by
   Anne Chambers, Wolfhound Press, 2003.

Hypatia: The Life and Legend of an Ancient Philosopher by
   Edward J. Watts, Oxford University Press, 2017.

A Radical Life: Biography of Megan Lloyd George by
   Mervyn Jones, Hutchinson, 1991.

If Not, Winter: Fragments of Sappho by Anne Carson,
   Virago, 2003.

Stung With Love: Poems and Fragments of Sappho by
   Carol Ann Duffy, Penguin Classics, 2009.
Suffragette: My Own Story by Emmeline Pankhurst, Vintage,
   2015.
Rise Up, Women!: The Remarkable Rise of the Suffragettes
   by Dr Diane Atkinson, Bloomsbury, 2018.
Frida: A Biography of Frida Kahlo by Hayden Herrera,
   HarperCollins, 1983.
*The Bride of Science: Romance, Reason and Byron's
   Daughter* by Benjamin Woolley, Macmillan, 1999.
Mekatilili Wa Menza: Woman Warrior by Elizabeth Mugi-
   Ndua, Sasa Sema Publications, 2000.
Departed But Not Forgotten: Women of China (series),
   Cheng & Tsui Co., 1984.
*Lives Like Loaded Guns: Emily Dickinson and Her Family's
   Feuds* by Lydall Gordon. Viking, 2010.
India's Bandit Queen: The True Story of Phoolan Devi by
   Mala Sen. Harvill Press, 1991.
Cleopatra: Last Queen of Egypt by Joyce Tyldesley, Profile
   Books, 2009.
The Collected Dorothy Parker by Dorothy Parker, Penguin
   Modern Classics, 2001.
Dorothy Parker: What Fresh Hell is This? by Marion
   Meade, Penguin, 1989.
Marie Stopes: A Biography by Ruth Hall, HarperCollins,
   1977.
Wanting by Richard Flanagan, Vintage, 2016, gives an
   unforgettable portrayal of the colonial treatment of
   Tasmania's Aboriginal people. Recordings of Fanny
   Cochrane-Smith's songs can be found online and are
   glorious.

305

Betty Ford: Candor and Courage in the White House by John Robert Greene, University Press of Kansas, 2004.

Mrs Beeton's Book of Household Management by Isabella Beeton, Empire Books, 2011.

The Short Life and Long Times of Isabella Beeton by Kathryn Hughes, HarperCollins, 2006.

The Transferred Life of George Eliot by Philip Davis, Oxford University Press, 2017.

Odette: World War Two's Darling Spy by Penny Starns, The History Press, 2009.

Sophia: Princess, Suffragette, Revolutionary by Anita Anand, Bloomsbury, 2015.

Game Changers: The Unsung Heroines of Sports History by Molly Schiot, Simon and Schuster, 2016.

The Match: Althea Gibson and the Portrait of a Friendship by Bruce Schoenfeld, Amistad Press, 2005.

Elizabeth: The Queen by Alison Weir, Vintage, 2009.

Elizabeth: Apprenticeship by David Starkey, Vintage, 2001.

Agatha Christie: A Biography by Janet Morgan, HarperCollins, 2017.

Broad Band: The Untold Story of the Women Who Made the Internet by Claire L. Evan, Portfolio, 2018. (For younger readers, try *Grace Hopper: Queen of Computer Code* by Laurie Wallmark, Sterling, 2017.)

Afghanistan: A Cultural and Political History by Thomas Barfield, Princeton University Press, 2012.

Catherine the Great by Robert K. Massie, Head of Zeus, 2012.

Catherine, Empress of All the Russias by Vincent Cronin, The Harvill Press, London, 1978.

Hedy's Folly: The Life and Breakthrough Inventions of Hedy Lamarr, the Most Beautiful Woman in the World, by Richard Rhodes, Doubleday, 2011.

Eleanor of Aquitaine: By the Wrath of God, Queen of England by Alison Weir, Pimlico, 2000.

Coco Chanel: The Legend and the Life by Justine Picardie, HarperCollins, 2013.

Nell Gwyn by Charles Beauclerk, Macmillan, 2005.

Rosalind Franklin: The Dark Lady of DNA by Brenda Maddox, HarperCollins, 2003.

The Double Helix: The Discovery of the Structure of DNA by James Watson, Weidenfeld & Nicholas, 2003.

Empress Dowager Cixi: The Concubine Who Launched Modern China by Jung Chang, Vintage, 2014.

Amelia Earhart: The Sound of Wings by Mary S. Lovell, Abacus, 2009.

Clara Schumann: The Artist and the Woman by Nancy B. Reich, Cornell University Press, 2001.

Inanna, Lady of the Largest Heart: Poems of the Sumerian High Priestess Enheduanna by Betty De Shong Meador, University of Texas Press, 2001.

Josephine Baker in Art and Life by Benetta Jules-Rosette, University of Illinois Press, 2007.

Victoria: A Life by A. N. Wilson, Atlantic, 2015.

The Wonderful Adventures of Mary Seacole in Many Lands by Mary Seacole, Penguin Classics, 2005.

Acknowledgements

This book came about because of many conversations with the amazing women we are lucky enough to know. Our publisher, Laura Hassan at Faber, has been an inspiration. We consider ourselves extremely lucky to have benefitted from her wit, wisdom and passion. We are also very grateful to the rest of the team at Faber: Lizzie Bishop, Lauren Nicoll, Niriksha Bharadia, Camille Morard, Emma Cheshire, Camilla Smallwood, Ella Griffiths, Pedro Nelson, Donna Payne, Kate Ward, Ian Critchley and Sarah Barlow. We are also grateful to Rosemary Davidson, Isabel Foley, Sophie Coates and, especially, Oliver Bebb and Jack Murphy.

MEMBERS

FABER

Become a Faber Member and discover the best in the arts and literature.

Sign up to the Faber Members programme and enjoy specially curated events, tailored discounts, and exclusive previews of our forthcoming publications from the best novelists, poets, playwrights, thinkers, musicians and artists.

ff